Praise for *New York Times* bestselling author

# JENNIFER LAUCK

## *SHOW ME THE WAY*

"A candid look at new motherhood. . . . [A] lucid, sympathetic, and often humorous portrayal of experiences to which many readers will be able to relate."

—*Booklist*

"Lauck is a gifted, engaging writer who leads readers to the busy intersection where parenting and personal history meet. While the details of Lauck's story are strikingly unique, every mother will identify with her unvarnished view of motherhood and with the self-discovery that awaits each parent."

—Amazon.com

## *STILL WATERS*

"Lauck's writing is admirably unadorned, never distracting attention from her gripping story."

—*The Washington Post*

"A perfectly pitched tale of survival and the courage to move on."

—*Kirkus Reviews*

## *BLACKBIRD*

"The unblinking look of one child at a hard world."
—Frank McCourt, author of *Angela's Ashes* and *'Tis*

"A standout."

—*Newsweek*

"A novelistic vision of a life with both hope and heartache to spare."

—*Harper's Bazaar*

Also by Jennifer Lauck
*Still Waters*
*Blackbird*

# Show Me the Way

## A Memoir in Stories

JENNIFER LAUCK

WASHINGTON SQUARE PRESS
New York London Toronto Sydney

Poem appearing on page 1 is from *American Primitive* by Mary Oliver. Copyright © 1978, 1979, 1980, 1981, 1982, 1983 by Mary Oliver; first appeared in *Yankee Magazine*. Courtesy of Little, Brown and Company, Inc.

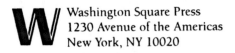

Washington Square Press
1230 Avenue of the Americas
New York, NY 10020

Copyright © 2004 by Jennifer Lauck

ISBN 978-0-7434-7639-3

First Washington Square Press trade paperback edition April 2005

10  9  8  7  6  5  4  3  2

Washington Square Press and colophon are registered trademarks of Simon & Schuster, Inc.

Manufactured in the United States of America

For information regarding special discounts for bulk purchases, please contact Simon & Schuster Special Sales at 1-800-456-6798 or business@simonandschuster.com

# ACKNOWLEDGMENTS

My circle of thanks begins with Atria Books, from sales to marketing to publicity, you are amazing souls and have said yes to me three times now. Thank you Judith Curr for leading the way and for all the flowers! Thank you Tracy Behar, your unflinching support soothed my soul. Another thank you for letting me stay with my dear friend and editor Kim Kanner Meisner.

Kimberly. Words cannot touch the thanks that live in my heart. Know this. We are kindred spirits.

Molly Friedrich. When we met, you predicted another baby would be in my future. You are a visionary, the best surrogate mother a motherless daughter could hope for and of course, a fantastic advocate and agent.

Mr. Tom Spanbauer. Your gift of craft and heart are the stuff of legend. Around your Dangerous Writing table with John, Robert, Liz, Joe, Martha, Jan, Kirk, Steve, Lisa, Kate,

Kathleen, Kai, Sage, Diane, and Diane, I found my heart (again). Thank you.

John. Fate, a well tuned guitar, a lithe pen, Rumi, Shakespeare, Rilke, trial and error, and open minds were the ingredients for an alchemy. Thank you, my friend.

Rhonda. Publisher of Hawthorne Books. Who can run two businesses and give me advice on the side? You. I'm in awe.

Hope. We ended up having babies a month apart and still wrote books and found time to offer each other comfort and advice. Thank you.

Steve. You always said: "If you're going to stand next to the fire, you have to be able to take the heat." You've stood next to mine longer than anyone now and have kept yourself from serious harm. You are a brave man. Thank you for your courage, for your confidence, and for tending my fire so well. Most of all, thank you for our beautiful children. Without you, there would be no story to tell.

Spencer and little Jo Jo, you deserve all my thanks. When the book is finally written on all of us, I hope I will have inspired you both as much as you have healed me.

*For The Dorseman*
*(AKA Steve)*

# CONTENTS

*Children are driven,*
*unconsciously,*
*in a direction*
*that is intended*
*to compensate*
*for everything*
*that was left*
*unfulfilled*
*in the life of their parents.*

—CARL JUNG

# PART ONE

# THE PAST

*. . . To live in this world*

*you must be able*
*to do three things;*
*to love what is mortal:*
*to hold it*

*against your bones knowing*
*your own life depends on it;*
*and, when the time comes, to let it go,*
*to let it go.*

—FROM *IN BLACKWATER WOODS*, MARY OLIVER

SHOW ME THE WAY

It's Mother's Day, actually Mother's Day night, and I lie in bed
with Steve. The windows are open, a row of three side by side,
and they are draped with linen sheers that dance on the air
of May.

Just outside, the wisteria and the lilac bloom purple. Out
front, the vines of the white roses tangle around the wood
pillars of the porch. Under today's long show of sun, hundreds
of those rosebuds burst open, bright white, as if they had a
secret they could no longer contain.

As I fall asleep, there are two things: the cool wind with its
smell of flowers and the feel of Steve, who breathes deep in
his chest on his inhales and lets out little puffs on his exhales.

Then there is something else.

I open my eyes.

Steve's on his back, his puffy breathing shifting into a low
snore.

I lie on my side with my legs and arms wound around a

3

pile of pillows and between my legs, there is a wet feeling like I just had an accident.

I roll out of the pillow nest and move the covers aside. I arch my back into the mattress and shove out of bed, stomach first.

I leave Steve and sleep behind, barefoot over the cool wood floors. A hairline of wet runs down the inside of my thigh.

In the bathroom, I close the door and snap on the light.

The white of the bulb makes my eyes burn.

I wad my nightgown in one hand and pull my underwear down with the other. I have to twist and bend to see past my stomach but down there, it's true. My underwear is soaked through.

I waddle-step myself to the toilet and sit down to get a closer look. The wet spot has no color I can see. I push my underwear off and kick it into the corner. I pull tissue off the roll, dab at myself, once, twice, three times and look at the wad in my hand. I dab again and look. There is no blood there at all, there's not even a shade of pink. It's just amniotic fluid, the bag of waters broken, the baby's indoor swimming pool with a hole in it and that's fine, except my baby isn't due for six more weeks.

I drop the wad of toilet paper into the toilet and rub my hands hard into my face, into my eyes. Black-and-white dots of nothing race wild inside my head.

In the dark of another night, I am seven years old and the heavy shake of a hand opens my eyes.

"Get up, Juniper," my father says.

He lets me go, stands up, and shakes B.J. where he sleeps on the top bunk of our beds.

"Wake up, son," my father says. "We've got to take your mom to a doctor."

Down the hall of our apartment, light spills out of their bedroom and my mother calls for my father in a voice that sounds broken.

He walks long steps out of our room and talks back at us.

"Come on, kids," he says, "get up now."

I get out of bed quick and take up pants folded neat at the end of the bed.

B.J. stays up there in his top bunk and rolls to face the wall.

He's always like that when we get woken up at night.

I snap my pants together and my hands shake hard. I run down the hall, pushing my nightgown into the waistband of my pants.

In their bedroom bathroom, my mother's crumpled on the floor with her bare legs out from her nightgown. She holds the toilet with both hands like she can't let go.

"Momma?" I say.

Her face is shaped like a heart and her eyes are as black as Egyptian stones. On her mouth, I can't tell if it's lipstick or blood. She wipes the red away with the back of her hand and searches for me as if I'm not right there.

I move in closer and when she sees me in the light, she smiles like this is fine, like everything is just fine.

This is fine, I tell myself, everything is just fine.

I flush the toilet and it takes the wadded tissues away.

The walls in our bathroom are a deep green and when we first painted this room, I dipped a duster into silver paint and

whispered the edges of feathers over the walls. It was something I read about in a book, this way to blend the seams
where plaster meets Sheetrock, but right now, closed in like I
am, it looks like some poor bird went insane.

I put my hands on the sink and the porcelain is cold on my
skin. In the mirror, my dark eyes are small in the pale of my
face and they have no idea what to do next.

All the books I have read say that when it's time for a
baby to come, there are contractions and pain, but I don't feel
anything.

I push off the sink and thump at my stomach like you'd
test a melon, my first finger firing off my thumb. The old
sound of being hollow in the center is gone. I move my hand
flat, touching the round shape that isn't so round anymore.
The skin of me shapes tight to the baby's form and without
water in there to help him float, his shoulders are all the way
down in my pelvis.

I hold myself around the bottom of my stomach.

"Move, baby, move."

My voice is loud in the crazy bird bathroom, but nothing
happens under my hands and quick, my mind swims to the
idea of how so many things can go wrong. Babies are born
dead or die minutes after or come with half a heart or only
one leg. It happens all the time.

I push my fingers deep enough into my pelvis to jog both
of us.

"Move!" I say.

There is nothing for a second, and then, he rolls against
my hand like, "Hey, I'm sleeping in here."

I pat against my stomach.

"That's fine," I say, "everything is going to be fine."

I go out of the bathroom then and turn on the overhead in our room. Bright light chases the night off Steve's bare shoulders and I go to his side of the bed.

I look at him with this idea that I should make this a sweet memory he'll never forget. I should be happy, giddy, thrilled. I should say, "Honey, wake up, our baby is coming."

I poke one finger into the muscle of his arm.

"Steve," I say.

His lashes lift a little.

I poke harder and Steve opens one eye.

"What?" he says.

I put both hands under the curve of my stomach.

"I think it's time."

Steve opens both of his eyes and sucks in a deep breath, lifting up on his elbow. He blinks himself awake and on his face is a look like he doesn't trust me.

"Are you kidding?"

I want to laugh, but can't get the sound up. I shake my head and hear myself talking fast enough to make it right.

"My water broke a few minutes ago, but there's no blood— I checked—and then I got the baby to move so I think it's fine, it's just early, that's all."

When I stop talking, he pulls himself up and his face is full of questions.

"What do we do now?" he says.


My father always knows what to do. He moves so sure and his voice is deep and strong, but I can tell he's scared too. It's there in how his dusty spice eyes move fast, how his voice is out of breath and how he pushes his hand through the thick of his dark hair over and over again.

He comes in the bathroom behind me and pushes his hair back on his head.

"Janet," he says, "we gotta go."

"No, Bud," my mother says. "I don't want to go."

Her smile is broken by a line of blood out the side of her mouth and blood swims in the toilet.

My father moves around me and lifts her off the floor.

She cries, "No, no, no," but he doesn't listen. He goes past me and out the bathroom door.

"Bring the blanket, Jenny," he says.

My father stops in the hall and yells.

"Bryan Joseph Lauck, get your butt out of bed."

I pull their throw blanket off the end of the bed and run after them.

"What about her robe?" I say.

My father takes her through the living room and his voice is so deep and so strong.

"Fine," he says, "bring her robe too."

Steve is clean-cut like the boy next door. He's got blue eyes, the baby face of innocence, and this confidence that comes from a life that hasn't hit him hard enough to fill him with doubt. He's not arrogant but he's on the edge of cocky, and if you ask, he'll give you advice on almost anything. What makes it worse is that most of the time he's right. Sometimes it bugs me that he knows everything, but right now I'd love a little advice. He looks like he wants the same thing from me though, and since it is my body, I figure it can't hurt to fake it for a while.

I put my hand on the cool skin of his shoulder and talk in a smooth voice that says I know more than I do.

"Why don't you call the doctor for me, ask her what we should do now and if this is a problem," I say, "and in the meantime, I'll double-check the book."

It's not much of a plan, but Steve nods like he's thankful for it. He throws the covers off his legs and goes downstairs, his bare feet slapping fast on the steps.

I go to the other side of the bed and get the bible of pregnancy, *What to Expect When You're Expecting*. I flip it open to the last chapter and the words read, "Water breaks. Go to the hospital. You're having a baby."

I let the book fold shut and toss it on the bed. I can't go anywhere without a bag.

Between my closet and the bathroom, I pull things together. There's a backpack for my stuff, extra underwear, clothes, a brush, my hair dryer, toothbrush, and a washcloth. I throw everything on the end of the bed and waddle myself into the nursery. In here, the crib is set against the wall, there's a mobile of dancing teddy bears over, and the window has teddy bear window shades to block out the light. I get a bag out of the closet and load it with a dozen tiny diapers, two outfits, a bib, another bib, a coat, a teddy bear, a jar of petroleum jelly, a tube of diaper ointment, and three blankets.

"Why are you packing all that stuff?" Steve says.

I almost jump out of myself, his voice is that much of a surprise, and I put my hands over my scared heart.

Steve stands at the door in his boxer shorts and on his face is the look he gets when he's pretty sure you're nuts, or at least doing something he can't understand.

The blankets I was trying to shove in fall on the floor.

I push my hand through my hair to calm myself since, honestly, I can't explain anything right now. I put one hand on the baby's dresser and pin a look on Steve instead.

"What did the doctor say?" I say.

Steve looks at the bag and rubs his hand over the whiskers on his face.

"We have to go to the hospital," he says.

"Did she say this is a problem?" I say. "Did she say it's too soon?"

"No," he says.

"No what?" I say.

I tilt my head to the side.

"No, it's not a problem?" I say. "Or no, it's not too soon, or what? Did you even talk to Dr. Bell?"

"I didn't talk to Dr. Bell," he says.

"Why not?"

"She's not on call."

"Who did you talk to?" I say.

"Another doctor, the one who is on call," he says.

"So why do we have to come in?" I say. "Is this like an emergency?"

"She didn't say that," Steve says.

"Well, what did she say?"

"To come in."

I stare him down hard as if more answers will come eventually, but he's a big fat blank. I throw my hands up in the air.

"Jeez, Steve," I say, "you didn't ask if it was too soon?"

"No," he says, "you just told me to call the doctor."

I wave him to get out of my way and he backs out of the doorway.

"I told you to ask if it was too soon," I say.

"No, you didn't," he says.

"Yes, I did," I say.

I push past him and go into our room.

"Why didn't you call them yourself?" he says.

"Forget it," I say, "I'll just look it up."

I dig my book from the pile of underwear and toiletries and flip to the chapter titled "34 Weeks." I'm shaking so hard, I have to hold my arm at the elbow while I read.

"At thirty-four weeks, your baby is almost fully formed and could be born with very few complications," I read.

I toss the book back on the bed and put my hands on my hips, as if I've made a major declaration. Steve looks at me, at the book on the bed and then at me again, and shakes his head.

"What does that mean?" he says.

Honestly, I don't know what it means, but I can't say that. I'm still faking it. I lean long over the bed instead and pull the backpack out of the pile of stuff.

"It means this is fine," I say. "Thirty-four weeks is fine, don't worry, everything will be fine."


In my mother's room, I get her robe off the floor and it's a puddle of white silk with purple flowers in the design. No matter how sick she is, her nightgowns always match her robes. My mother is always in style.

B.J. is in the living room with his jeans pulled up but not zipped, and he wrestles with a wadded-up T-shirt. He goes slow out the door, T-shirt over his head, and he pushes his arms through the arm holes, only he moves like it's Sunday morning and we have all day to play.

Behind him, my head is about to explode from how slow he goes.

"Come on," I say, "move it!"

B.J. stops cold and I stop just short of mashing up against his back. He puts a hand on the jamb to block me. His dark hair is over at the wide angle of his side part and his dark eyes stare me down.

"You move," B.J. says.

Outside, the car door slams and my father goes around his low-slung sports car to open his own door.

"Goddammit, you kids, let's go already," he yells from the street and I can see him out there through the gate of B.J.'s arm.

B.J. looks at me for a long time and right then, I want to be as big as he is. I want to kick the shit out of him, except part of me knows he's not mad at me. He's seen all of this before and more; hospital runs, waiting in the car, operations and pills for the voices she says she hears in the night. He's tired and he's given up, it's right there in the dark of his eyes that are so much different than mine. I've seen a lot too, I've seen almost everything that he has seen, but I'm not like that. I never give up.

I shove past him and the slick of her robe gives just enough slide to get by. He hits me up the back of my head, just barely, just enough to hurt, but it's fine. I'm free to run to the car where my father waits, free not to look back, free not to care.

\*          \*          \*

When Steve and I leave, it's past one in the morning and Mother's Day is over. My back hurts low down deep, but it's not terrible. It's more like being squeezed too hard.

In the car, we've packed the baby car seat, the baby bag, a CD player Steve gave me this morning for my first Mother's Day, and a whole stack of music for the right background sound. We've got extra water, extra juice in a cooler, and I even have my favorite pillow. As we leave, though, it feels like I've left something behind.

Steve backs down our long driveway and I watch out the window.

Our house lifts in the night, just right with its three coats of fresh paint, its windows that have been washed, and its driveway that's been swept clean. Inside is just as nice with more fresh paint, new pipes, and wood floors that shine like spilled honey. It's a safe-and-perfect-from-the-outside house to fit our safe-and-perfect-from-the-outside life to fit Steve who is safe-and-perfect-from-the-outside too. He's ready for all this, he's always wanted to be a husband, a homeowner, and a father. I thought I was ready too. I wanted to be ready, but deep down I don't think I'm ready. I'm not strong enough. I don't think I can do it. I want this baby, I do, but something is missing inside of me.

Steve pulls out of the driveway and onto the street.

A deep pain digs at my back and catches my breath. I want to keep looking back, but I can't anymore.

I move myself in the seat to face front and Steve puts his hand on my leg.

"Are you okay?" he says. "Is it a contraction?"

I shake my head no, I'm not okay, and nod my head yes, it's a contraction.

\*          \*          \*

My father's car is so small, being in the backseat is almost like being in the front seat. In the back, I hold my father's seat with both my hands and I can see my mother slumped down. Her eyes are closed.

B.J. is wedged tight next to me and his leg and shoulder are pressed against mine. He keeps shoving against me and I shove back.

My father drives fast and the sound of the engine is deep into my body, like a very big man clearing his throat for a long time.

I ignore B.J. and keep my eye on her. Even now, like this, she's so beautiful it hurts. Her dark hair is curled around her heart of a face and there is something about the fine lines of her bones that make her a woman, but also a little girl, like me.

She's been sick as long as I can remember. She's walked with crutches, two, then one, then none. She's gone away, come back and gone away again, and had operations on places I can't understand. One time, she lifted her nightgown so I could see her whole stomach. It was a wicked mess of sliced and sewn lines, a tic-tac-toe where no one ever won.

"I hate doctors," she said, "they never seem to get it right."

I touched over those scars and traced her lines and I hated doctors too. I hated how they cut her so many times. I hated how they forced a tube between her legs that pulled urine into a bag she kept on the floor. I hated how they gave her so many different pills, poisons that made her sleep, and made her talk in circles and even made her mad enough to give up on her life on the day she tried to overdose.

My father makes a hard left into the driveway where a bright red sign reads EMERGENCY.

He stops the car hard, gets out, and runs around to her side of the car. He opens the door and kneels down to take her to his chest. He looks at B.J. and me in the back, dusty spice eyes back and forth between us.

"Stay put," he says. "I'll be right back."

"Okay," I say, except I can't hear my own voice.

He lifts her then and she's liquid in his arms, the white of her skin a strange white turning blue. He carries her into the hospital and the blanket drags on the ground. I watch until I can't see them anymore.

B.J. leans over the seat and shoves the latch to get it forward. He gets himself out, shoves the seat back hard, and sits down in the front.

I want to say that we're not supposed to move, but B.J.'s so mad, he'll sock me for sure.

I shift myself around to be just me in the back, getting myself situated the way I do in the middle, and I wipe the feel of B.J. off my arm and leg. My hands hurt from holding on to my father's seat so hard and I open them, close them, and open them again.

Down at my feet is her white robe with the purple flowers. I put my hands deep into the cold silk and try to feel her there, except she's gone.

My eyes sting the way they do when I'm about to cry and I put my face into the silk, pressing so hard I won't make a sound.


Steve turns into the driveway of St. Vincent's Hospital and backs into a regular spot close to the front door. It's a big rectangle of a building with those reflective windows that mirror the night, the trees on the grounds, and the cars in the parking lot. From the inside, people can see out, but from the outside I can't see in.

Steve takes the keys out of the ignition and it's quiet in the car.

"You okay?" he says.

I nod at the windshield.

"Yeah," I say, "I'm fine."

"Are you sure?" he says.

"Yes," I say, "I'm fine."

"You don't look fine," Steve says, "you look a little scared."

He watches me the way he does, eyes digging deep. I hate how he does that, it's like being pushed at all the time and the truth is, I've already told him I'm scared about a lot of things, especially of being here.

I wanted a home birth, I wanted the quiet and calm that comes from home. I wanted my things around me and maybe some nice music.

Steve went white on that idea.

He said, "People have babies in hospitals."

He said, "Our insurance covers a doctor and hospital."

He said, "What if something goes wrong?"

He said, "What if we need a doctor?"

Steve talked me into a hospital. We even took a tour with a nurse disguised as a tour guide.

She took us to a room called a suite and showed off all the amenities. She was a pretty woman gone soft with a blond helmet of hair she had trained to flip out in one round curl.

"You have plenty of space," she said, "and there's a refrigerator under this counter too."

I stayed by the door of the room, ready to go, but Steve

was in there checking out everything. He took a remote control off the side table near the mechanical bed and waved it in my direction.

"Look, Jen," Steve said, "cable TV."

The nurse patted a makeshift sofa under the window.

"And there's a little fold-out bed for you, Dad," she said.

Steve hooked his head like I should come in and take a look.

The nurse chattered away, blond hair lifting and falling around her shoulders, and turned on a computer next to the bed.

I walked in with slow steps and opened a cabinet over the sink. Inside were sterile packages of tubes and needles.

The nurse said they had the latest technology and could monitor the baby's heartbeat with straps that hooked me to the computer.

I closed the cabinet door and opened the bathroom door. There was a stand-up shower with a seat for people who probably couldn't stand on their own and there was a stack of heavy-duty maxi pads on a shelf.

"How many babies are born here a month?" Steve said.

"About four hundred," she said.

"Wow," Steve said. "That's big business."

I closed the bathroom door.

The nurse tapped at the keys on the computer and nodded like she agreed.

In my head, I did the math of four hundred babies a month at about five thousand per baby. It was a lot of money. It was enough money to make them disguise the place as a hotel and cover up how it was really big business corporate bullshit messing with my body. I was getting myself pissed off enough and working up the courage to say, "Forget this, I'm having my baby at home." I even crossed my arms under my boobs and rested them over the rise of my stomach, but then I saw it there. Nailed to the wall next to me was a crucifix, this tiny version of the savior's suffering cast in chipped bronze.

A crucifix within twenty feet made me straighten my spine and snap into the form of an obedient daughter. I uncrossed my arms.

The nurse stopped with the computer and tiptoed to a shelf, taking a bunch of papers down. She gave most of the pages to Steve, saying that we could read over the materials and call with any questions. One of the pages she handed my way.

"This is for your birth plan," she said.

I took the page of pink paper with baby feet faded into the background.

"Fill that out and bring it when you come to have your baby," she said. "It gives us a way to help you have the kind of birth you want."

Steve rolled his stack of papers into a cone and nodded in his big way that said he thought a birth plan was a great idea. Most of the time, I loved him for being so optimistic and for trying to make me optimistic too, but something in me just couldn't give in this time.

"If I fill this out," I said, "the birth will go the way I want?"

"You bet," she said.

I waved the page and the paper rippled in the air.

"If I write that I don't want drugs or any intervention at all," I said, "that's how the birth will go?"

The nurse pushed her hands into the front pockets of her top, this smock-style thing in a pastel color that matched the birthing suite walls, and she looked at Steve for a translation.

"She wants to do this all natural," Steve said.

The tone of his voice said, "I have no idea what she's thinking." The nurse lifted her eyebrows like she understood him perfectly.

She leaned my way, her nurse shoes squeaky on the linoleum floor, and patted a cool hand on my arm.

"Don't you worry," she said, "we are here to help you have the birth you want."

In the reflection of the hospital windows, I can see Steve and me in our car. We look so small. We look even smaller compared to the size of the hospital. I wonder if Steve sees how small we are. I wonder if he's ever felt this scared. But that's not Steve's way and if I tell him how scared I am, he'll just shake me off, or worse, think that I'm weak. Steve's strong and he admires people who are that way too. I can do strong just as well as anyone else.

I pull the handle of my door.

"I'm not scared, Steve," I say. "Let's just get this thing over with."

My stomach leads the way out of the car and I slam the door, opening the back to get out my bag.

Steve comes around fast.

"I've got this stuff," he says.

"I've got it," I say.

I pull the bag by the strap, but he grabs it away before I can get it to my shoulder.

"Just let me do this, Jen," he says.

He moves the bag over his own shoulder and takes a couple more things out of the car.

I stand there for a second with nothing in my hand, but as he goes by, I snap an envelope out of the side pocket of my pack.

Steve's irritated, it's right there in how he walks ahead of me, taking long, sure steps to the front door.

I lag behind and hold the envelope on the curve of my stomach. Inside is my birth plan with simple words that add up to: No drugs, no intervention, no IVs, and no heartbeat monitors that will strap me down in the bed indefinitely.

In the hospital lobby, Steve stops at a desk made of dark wood and talks to someone. He's leaned on one elbow, feet crossed at the ankle and my bag slung over his shoulder so casual, he may as well be checking into a hotel.

I don't go in though. I stand on the plastic ramp of the automatic doors and they stay open with my weight pressed down.

It doesn't matter how casual Steve is about this whole thing, I know where we are. I know this is a place where life and death come through the same door. I know that when I come out, if I come out, I'm not going to be the same. Nothing is ever going to be the same.

Steve looks back like I'm right behind him, but no one is there and he finds me at the door. He shakes his head and opens his hand like, "What are you doing?"

One step at a time, I come the rest of the way in and that fast, the doors close behind me with a loud sucking sound, like God taking a deep breath.


On the other side of the EMERGENCY door, there is the white light of the hospital and people who walk back and forth in white clothes.

My father comes out of the doors and pushes his hand through his dark hair.

Her robe is still in my lap and the dried salt of tears make the skin on my face tight.

My father gets in the car, shuts the door, and looks straight into the night.

"It's okay now," he says, "they'll take good care of her."

He leans over the gear shifter and flips open the door of the glove compartment.

B.J. shifts his knees to make room while my father digs out his Pall Malls. After he gets them, B.J. shuts the glove compartment door.

My father sets himself straight again and shakes the pack a little, taking a smoke up between his lips.

B.J. pushes in the plug of the lighter and when it pops out, my father lights his cigarette. He hands the lighter back to B.J., who puts it back into that little hole in the dashboard by the radio dials.

My father smokes and starts the car, B.J. slouches low in his seat and looks out the window. I'm dying for talk, for words that make sense, for something that will explain what is going on, but the two of them are up there in their silent world of men. I watch the hospital as we drive away, and a hundred questions are trapped in my head.

At the front desk, the nurse is young and fresh. She talks in a high, little girl voice and has this habit of tucking her hair behind her ears even though it's short.

She puts together a pile of papers, clips them to a clipboard, and hands it over to Steve.

"You fill this out, Dad," she says, "and you come with me, Mom."

Steve puts our stuff on the floor near the check-in desk and takes the clipboard. I stay next to him, the envelope against my stomach and I smooth it flat as if it got wrinkled.

"Do I give you my birth plan?" I say, "or should I hold it for someone else?"

The nurse stands with this bouncy little move, tucks her hair behind her ears, and puts her hand out palm up.

"I'll take it," she says.

The paper is warm from my touch and I offer it her way. For a second, I almost snap it back, but she takes it out of my hand and puts it on the desk.

She doesn't open it or even look, she just drops the envelope and waves for me to follow her.

My envelope is so white against the dark wood of the desk, and I watch it even as I walk away.

"Are you having any contractions?" the nurse says.

She stands at the open door of a small examining room and I go in, pushing into the low of my back.

"I'm having a lot of pain here," I say.

The nurse closes the door and digs under the examining table.

"It catches my breath, but then goes away," I say.

She pulls out two folds of fabric and tosses them on a table covered with white paper.

"Go ahead and get changed," she says.

She pulls a big machine out from the corner of the room and plugs it into the wall. The machine makes this beeping sound and she taps on some keys on a keyboard.

The nurse looks up at me, a little surprised, and nods at the gowns again.

"Go ahead and get changed," she says, "we're going to look at the baby on an ultrasound and then we need to start an IV of antibiotics and saline."

Weak in my legs, I lean into the examining table, and hold my stomach.

"I don't want any IVs," I say, "it's on my plan. No drugs."

The computer flashes lights and the nurse does her little hair tuck behind her ears.

"Your doctor already called," she says, nodding as she talks, "she gave me instructions to start an IV of antibiotics."

"Why?" I say.

"For an infection," she says. "Your water broke early and that may be due to an infection."

I stand on both feet again.

"I don't have any infection," I say.

"You might," she says.

"I don't," I say. "I know I don't."

She sits with her hands on her knees. So young. So fresh.

"I want my husband in here with me," I say.

She tucks her hair behind her ears.

"All right," she says. "I'll get him, but maybe you can get changed?"

"Fine," I say.

She gets up bouncy but not as bouncy as before.

"Be right back," she says.

"Great," I say.

When she leaves, it's just me in the room and I let out a deep breath. I take off my sweatpants, my T-shirt, and a big denim shirt, peeling the warm layers of me away to become a pile on the floor. I shake open what's supposed to be a gown, but it's so thin there's no way to feel warm inside it.

There's a knock on the door and Steve is in the door crack with questions in his blue eyes.

"What's wrong?" he says.

I tug the material of the gown over my behind and pull the door open. The nurse is back in the shadows of the hall. I pull him in and close the door on her.

"They want to put me on an IV," I say. "I don't want any drugs."

Steve nods like he knows and talks slow like I might not understand if he spoke more quickly.

"Jen," he says, "you have to think about the baby now, these people are here to help you."

I take his hand and hold his fingers tight.

"Honey, I don't have an infection," I say, "I just had a test for that."

"You did?" he says.

"Yes," I say, "on Friday and this is Sunday. There's no way I got an infection in two days. There's just no way."

My confidence shifts him back to my side and he nods like this makes sense.

After that, the nurse calls my doctor to ask about the test, but she has to leave a message with some service.

While we wait for the callback, the nurse squeezes goo on my stomach and moves a paddle around to see how the baby looks on ultrasound. He's curled up tight and low in my pelvis, positioned just the way he's supposed to be.

Steve has a happy, ready-to-be-a-dad smile on his face.

"This is a big baby for thirty-four weeks," the nurse says.

She looks over my file, her finger moving down some chart.

"It says here that you conceived in September? September nineteenth?" she says. "Are you sure it wasn't more like August?"

The date a baby is due is based on the first day of a woman's last period. You take that day, put it on a wheel, spin out forty weeks, and presto, you've got a due date. I know we got pregnant on September 19th, but I don't want to explain it here. Steve knows I don't want to explain too and he smiles his best smile at the nurse, the one that melts hearts.

"We got pregnant the first month we tried," Steve says, "we're very sure it was September."

The nurse giggles at Steve, charmed. She tucks her hair behind her ear.

"Okay," she says.

On September 19th, B.J. turns ten years old and he gets to wish for anything. His wish has two parts. First he wants breakfast at the International House of Pancakes and second, he wants to see our mother.

When he says his birthday wish out loud, my father's whole face frowns into deep lines around his eyes and into his forehead.

"You're still not old enough to go in," my father says, "you know that, don't you, buddy?"

B.J. nods like yes, he knows.

"I just want to be there." he says, "We'll wait in the car and you can go tell her it's my birthday."

My father moves his whole hand over his face and works his fingers around his jawline.

"She knows it's your birthday," my father says. "She'd want you to go somewhere fun, like the beach or maybe on a sailing trip."

B.J. shakes his head at those ideas.

"I just want to go to the hospital," B.J. says.

My father moves his jaw around like he's setting himself straight.

It's so odd, a birthday wish wasted on pancakes and an afternoon of sitting in a parking lot and it's even more odd because B.J.'s not that way. He's never talked about her while she's been gone and the whole thing makes me feel strange in my stomach.

My father pushes his hand through his hair then and his dusty eyes look sad.

"Okay, B.J.," he says. "We'll go see your mom."


My doctor calls back and says the test I took last Friday doesn't matter. She doesn't want to take any chances. She says I can have a shot instead of an IV, but no matter what, I have to take antibiotics.

The nurse says the shot hurts a lot, but I don't care, the shot will be over and I won't have any tubes stuck in my body afterward.

The nurse comes in with a tray and two huge hypodermic needles. They are big enough for cows.

"Are you sure you don't want an IV?" the nurse says.

I can't take my eyes off those needles but nod my head yes, I'm sure.

I turn myself around and lean over on the table. The nurse

moves my gown a little, rubs my skin with a pad of alcohol, and I lean all my weight on my elbows.

Steve sits in a chair by the door and I hold on to his blue eyes, to his innocence, to his confidence, as if those elements of him will have strength enough for me.

The needle pushes in and I close my eyes on Steve. There's a deep sting and then, down my leg, a run of pain so powerful, so intense, my knees give in. Steve is up to catch me as I go down and he grabs me under my elbows.

"Jen," he says, "hold on."

The drug moves slow and thick in my blood and it feels like something is ripping my leg off my body.

I lean so heavy into Steve he has to shift himself to hold my weight. I feel like I'm leaving this place, this black of nothing in my head.

"How often do you have to give her those?" I hear Steve say.

"Every four hours," the nurse says.

An hour later, I'm in one of the pastel blue suites, strapped to the bed by a baby heartbeat monitor and two IVs are in my arms. The tubes are attached to needles stuck into veins in my wrist and held in place with clear plastic tape. I guess the IVs aren't as bad as the shot, but they still hurt like hell.

My birth plan? I have no idea. It could be in that envelope abandoned on the front desk, or maybe by now it's been fed into a shredder somewhere, the sound of the machine drowning out the sound of nurses laughing at the stupid woman who didn't want any drugs.

Steve is gone somewhere too, checking out this part of the birthing wing, and I roll my head on the pillow. The machine

I'm attached to beeps and there are numbers on a red screen that are the baby's heartbeat. They read 144, 145, 146. The sound from the machine is steady and strong.

Steve comes through the door and he's got two plastic cups in his hands.

"This is great," he says, "they've got all the soda you can drink at a courtesy bar down the hall."

He puts a cup down next to the bed.

"I got you a Sprite," he says.

From the cup comes the bubbly sound of carbonation and he sips at his own cup, watching me over the rim.

"I got Coke," he says.

I wish I could throw the Sprite into his face and scream at him, but I don't. I just smile and nod like, "Great—soda."

There's a knock at the door and a woman pushes past the curtain that hangs in front of the door.

"Are you the Laucks?" she says.

Steve doesn't share my name, but he nods anyway, yes, we're the Laucks, and she comes in. She's got a clipboard under her arm, a stethoscope around her neck, and she's wearing blue pants and a blue top. There's a nametag pinned to her top, but I cannot deal with who she is. I just look at her face that's long and pointy like a greyhound dog.

She talks to us in a flat monotone of a voice, announcing she's from the intensive care unit and that she's here to prepare us for what could happen with a premature baby.

She holds the clipboard in her arms and the sound of her voice is lost in the beep of the baby's heartbeat.

"He might not be able to breathe," she says.

"His heart may stop," she says.

"You may not be able to take him home for at least six weeks," she says.

Steve puts his soda down next to mine and crosses his arms over himself to take the blows of her bad news. The more she talks, the more still he gets, the color gone from his face. Steve turns into a rock.

I feel like I'm not even in the room with them. I float high above the whole scene and watch these poor fools bumble around.

"Any questions?" the nurse says.

She stands there waiting and Steve's stunned quiet makes me come back, makes me clear my throat.

"What are the chances he'll be fine?" I say.

The nurse tilts her head like she doesn't understand me.

"Fine?" she says.

I push my hands into the soft of the bed and adjust myself to sit up a little taller.

"Fine," I say. "You know, normal and healthy, able to go home."

The nurse looks down at her clipboard for such a long time, perhaps at the shreds of my birth plan, and then she sets her sights on Steve, as if he's the more reasonable of the two of us.

"I wouldn't count on anything," she says, "it's best to be prepared."

Steve pushes through his hair, this slow move of a man who looks like he's in over his head.

I can't go where he's going, I can't even let myself imagine the kind of things she's talking about. I can't think that way and have a baby.

I look at the heartbeat machine instead and meditate on the numbers that go up and down between 144 and 147.

Steve asks a few more questions, more doom and gloom. I don't have any questions. It's quiet in the room for a long time and when I feel her leave, I look down at my own hands held together on my lap. I move my wedding ring around my finger and whatever labor pains I had are gone now, chased away by the shot and the IVs and by just being in a hospital.

"She's wrong," I say to my hands.

"What?" Steve says.

I shift off my hands and onto his scared face. "She's wrong," I say.

"How do you know?" Steve says.

"I know," I say.

"How?" he says.

This is how it is between Steve and me. We don't speak the same language. He's all about facts and what you can touch and see. I believe in those things too, but there's more. There's always been more. I know certain things in my heart. My problem is that I haven't learned how to speak my language very well, at least in a way that can convince a person like Steve, or that stupid nurse, of my meaning.

I move my hand over my stomach and the tubes pull pain against my wrist.

"I just know," I say.

Steve licks his lips and pushes his hands into the pockets of his jeans.

"I mean it," I say, "she's wrong."

I nod at the machine, at the numbers that stay steady and strong.

"Just look at his heart, look how strong he is."

Steve puts his hand on top of the machine and looks at the numbers for a long time.

I don't know what he sees in those numbers, I can't read his mind, but it doesn't matter. I know what I know.

I lie back in the bed then and pull the covers up over my legs. I close my eyes and the only sound is the beep of our baby's heart.


At the IHOP my father eats slow and orders cup after cup of coffee. When it's finally time, he pays the bill and the three of us go out to where the car is parked.

Outside, it's hot and sunny, but it's always that way. L.A. is sunshine and palm trees. It's like a vacation that never ends.

Before he gets in, my father leans his elbows on the roof of the car and talks over the top. He's got a toothpick in his mouth and it moves up and down with his words.

"Are you sure you don't want to go to the beach?" he says.

B.J. goes around to the passenger side, a toothpick in his mouth too.

"Yep," B.J. says.

The two of them consider each other and then my father takes the toothpick out of his mouth and tosses it on the ground. He opens his door for me and I climb in under his arm.

"We could drive over to Anaheim and take in Disneyland," my father says, "and then stop by on the way back."

B.J. climbs in front and slams his door.

"Nope," B.J. says.

My father shuts his door and he looks over at B.J., who's

slouched low in his seat, working his toothpick. He starts up the car and revs the engine a couple times.

In the tape deck, a man sings.

*I'm looking for a hardheaded woman, one who will make me do my best. If I find my hardheaded woman, I know the rest of my life will blessed.*

We drive then, in the direction of the hospital, and I watch the palm trees out the window, lined up so perfect along the sidewalks.

I like that song. I like to think about me growing up to be one of those hardheaded women, a woman who will know things that other people don't know, a woman who has all the answers.

I stand in front of the baby heart monitor and watch the numbers that beat out the same song, 144, 145, 146.

It's Wednesday night, three nights after my water first broke, and Steve went home to get some sleep. A nurse came in a while back, put a fat new bag of antibiotics on the hook, and started up another of saline. She said she was going home. She said a new nurse would check on me in a couple of hours.

I have on two gowns now, one like a robe, the other like a nightgown, but I don't remember the last time I was really warm.

I move my hand over my stomach and it's tight and heavy.

Past the machine, another crucifix is nailed to the wall.

When we first got here, I wanted to take it down and put it into a drawer. I didn't do it though. Something like that has to be a huge sin.

I look at it now, really look.

The crucifix is small, maybe as big as my own hand, and the mini Jesus who hangs there is dead at this point, or pretty close. Even though he's tiny, I can still make out the detail of his long angled face, his beard, and the wavy hair on his head. His eyes are closed, he's got a tiny nose, and his lips are pressed together. I touch my finger to his arms spread wide on the cross, touch all the way to the tip of one hand and press into the tiny nail that holds him down.

In these three days, I have seen six doctors, that many nurses, and heard twice as many opinions.

They have given me drugs to force labor and then stopped the drugs, worried that my uterus would bleed out.

They have given me drugs to soften my cervix, but my body isn't doing anything.

Steve has lost all respect for this place.

"These doctors are like bad mechanics," he says. "They tinker around under the hood, but they don't know much about fixing a problem."

Again, he's right. Even the doctors admit they can try this or do that, but in the end it's up to the mysterious chemistry between my body and the baby.

My finger moves over the rise of tiny rib bones and whoever made this crucifix even put the two small slashes into Jesus' chest, the ones that were cut into him as he hung there on the cross. It's the part of the story that always got to me. The man was already nailed to the cross and dying under the brutal heat of the sun. Why cut his flesh? Why make him suffer so?

Our insurance company keeps calling, wondering why I haven't had the baby yet and somewhere the cost of all this is being added up. I have a feeling the insurance company will

be pushing for a C-section pretty soon. I have a feeling my
time is running out.

I touch all the way down to the tips of Jesus' toes and my
finger catches on the nail that holds him down.

Since I have been in this hospital, my blood has been
drawn three times. Each time, the white blood count goes
down, which means no infection, no infection, no infection.
I've known it all along. I also know that I'm never going to
have this baby with all this crap pumping into me.

My God, my God, why have You forsaken me, I think
those were the last words of Jesus before he died. What kind
of God does such a thing to His only son? Why is that love?
And what about Mary? Why is she down there at her son's feet
letting him die such a terrible death? Is that what being a
mother is? Are we expected to let some God torture our child
and call it love? Is this what I believe in?

I stop touching Jesus then and hold myself instead, my
hands cupped around my own son locked inside. Across the
room, I see myself reflected in the window, this woman heavy
with a baby that just won't come.

I've been to church enough to be afraid of God and to
learn the lesson that I'm nothing but a woman in a permanent state of sin, but what about this slice of heaven inside
of me? If I can make life in my own body, can't I make a decision for myself, can't I trust what I know? But then, what if
I make a mistake? How will I ever forgive myself if something goes wrong, but at the same time, how much longer
can I go on like this, waiting for other people to show me
the way?

When you look at a thing long enough, it can almost
change form. That's how it is with the crucifix. It's really just a

tiny man nailed to a cross. That was two thousand years ago and this is now. I don't have to be obedient. I don't have to be good. I just have to do what I'm here to do.

I take a deep, deep breath and pull the strap of the heart-beat monitor. The Velcro makes a ripping sound and the monitor goes flat.

I roll the tubes and belt up, shoving everything on a shelf under the machine. I'm a little lost without the beeping sound and the run of numbers 144, 145, and 146. There's doubt in the quiet and even a little fear.

I hear the sound of nurses out in the hall, voices talking as they change shifts. I wheel the IV stand across the room and the plastic tubes swing between my wrist and the bags. I close the door of my room and go into my bathroom, closing that door too. I push the lock on the knob and it makes a small click.

The bathroom is small with brown tile on the floor, on the walls, even on the ceiling. I stand on tiptoe and take the bag of antibiotics off the hook. There's a small plug in the bottom of the bag and I hold the whole thing over the toilet and pull. The antibiotics spit into the toilet and I force all of it out, every last little bit, and then put the plug back into the bottom. I hang it up again and do the same thing with the saline.

In the mirror, I don't recognize myself. My face is fat and puffy from all the drugs and my skin is the pasty white of someone who hasn't slept or eaten in three days.

I turn the shower on, adjusting the water to be so hot that the room fills fast with steam. I get myself out of both gowns, twisting and turning to separate fabric from the tubes still attached to my arms.

In the mirror, the steam takes my image away or at least my clarity, but I am still there, big and naked and full. I move my hands down the sides of my stomach, down low to where I can feel his shoulders resting.

It's time, little man, let's go.

I step in the shower, hot water washing me down, and I pull the curtain closed.


I don't know why, but B.J. and I fight all the time. It's this thing in the air between us, this snap that waits until we are alone and when we are, he punches me and I kick to get away.

He's in front but turned around with his chest against the seat, arms swinging and I'm in the back, kicking against his fists.

My father pounds his hand on the roof of the car and I can hear him yell at us from outside. B.J. turns around quick and I pull my legs to be crossed.

"Knock it off," my father says, opening the door fast. "Stop hitting your sister. What's the matter with you?"

My father gets into the car and shuts his door hard.

"She started it," B.J. says.

"Did not," I say.

"Did too," B.J. says.

My father puts his hand up between us.

"Enough," my father says.

B.J. shifts around to face front.

"How is she?" B.J. says.

My father goes from being angry to happy that fast and makes his biggest smile, all teeth and squinty eyes.

"Great," he says.

"Did she say anything about my birthday?" B.J. says.

"Sure did," my father says. "I'll tell you everything when we get home."

He starts up the car then and there's something in the way he talks. It's different for him.

"Is she coming home?" I say.

"Is she coming home today?" B.J. says.

My father shakes his head like that's not it.

"I'll tell you when we get home," he says.

An hour after I pour out the antibiotics, I go into real labor.

Before, it just felt like some squeezing around my back, but that went away after the shot from hell. Later, when I was on something called Pitocin, I felt like I was getting kicked in the back. Now, I'm being pulled into a hole of pain that can't breathe and the only way up and out of the hole is to make myself suck air in. It helps to make a deep sound too. I make the sound from the deepest center of my core, this low, hard moan. If I heard it outside of myself, I'd think some poor animal was dying somewhere.

I rock in a chair, moaning that way, and fall into a kind of sleep where I dream I'm not in pain. When I wake from the dream, there is the hospital room, the rocking chair, and Steve, who sits close and gives me a cup of water with a straw.

If I'm not rocking and moaning and sleeping, I'm in the shower being sprayed low on my back. Steve holds the nozzle on me while I stand with my hands pressed into the wall, my face into my arm.

The nurse keeps coming in, telling me to get out of the

shower to check the baby's heartbeat, and I do it as long as I can and then I get back in the shower.

People keep trying to talk to me, asking me questions about what I'd like to do.

"Do you want a narcotic for the pain, or how about that epidural?"

It hurts to think. It hurts almost as bad as the pain that's low in my groin and I say no through the hours until I can't take it anymore. Twelve hours later, I finally say yes to anything that will get me out of this pain, but then the nurse looks inside me and says it's time.

I'm ten centimeters dilated and that's the magic number.

The suite is unfolded to become one hundred percent hospital room. The bed breaks into two pieces, the bottom half wheeled away and two metal bars for pushing are folded up by my hips. From behind a mirror, a table is folded down and a nurse sets it up with sterile instruments, gloves, and masks. Someone turns a switch and these high beam lights that were hidden in the ceiling shine white between my legs. A doctor comes in then, a woman I've never met, and sits in a stool that's waiting at the end of the bed.

She says something to me, but her voice is trapped behind her mask.

"What?" I say.

"Olsen," Steve says, "she's Dr. Olsen."

"Oh," I say.

As if I still have any say, I lean up on my elbows and look her square into her eyes, the only part of her I can see.

"Don't cut me," I say.

"You don't want an episiotomy?" she says.

"That's right," I say, "help me do this without cutting me."

She nods like she understands.

Two nurses are behind her, strangers from the intensive care unit, and Steve takes his place on one side; a nurse named Jackie waits on the other.

The doctor looks around at all of us, like the coach of a team ready to play the big game.

"All right," the doctor says, "let's have a baby."

Steve has set up the CD player and it's Seal singing smoky and deep, a song called "Show Me." The lyrics are, *Show me the way to solve your sorrows and I'll do what I can.*

My father won't say anything until we get all the way back to our apartment and when we get there, we have to go inside too.

We live up a steep hill and our living room window faces the ocean. You can see all of it from up here. You can see the wide blue water, the white caps, and even the little sailboats way out in the distance.

"Let's sit, guys," my father says.

He points us to a round purple sofa.

"Jennifer," Dr. Olsen says, "you have to hold your breath for ten seconds and then let it go."

"Okay," I say.

I take a deep breath and Steve and Jackie press me forward.

I hold my breath and Dr. Olsen counts while I push.

"One, two, three," she says.

When we sit down, we face out to the ocean. B.J. is on one side of my father and I'm on the other. My father puts his arms around both of us and the weight of him is heavy on my shoulders.

*          *          *

"Eight, nine, ten," Dr. Olsen says.

Steve and Jackie lay me back, but I don't want to be back, I just want to push again.

"Take another deep breath," Dr. Olsen says, "you are very close."

I suck in all the air I can and sit up, bearing down against the press of Dr. Olsen's hand between my legs.

Everyone in the room says, "Push, push, push."

"Your mother died this morning," my father says.

I push so hard it hurts and burns between my ears and I hear myself scream, "Get this baby out of me!"

"It's better this way," my father says, "she was in so much pain."

He says more, but I can't hear his words. Instead, I bend against my knees and over there, B.J.'s face is gone to shadow like a cloud passed in front of the sun. He knew. He knew all along and he didn't even know he knew.

"One more push," Dr. Olsen says.

I hold my breath like I will never breathe again and push.

Through the center of me, a baby comes into our world, a tiny old man with his arms crossed over his chest.

The ocean rises and falls, so big and blue and forever out there, and I sit back. I never felt her leave. I felt her coming home instead. I feel her close right now. I smell her almond lotion and her Parliaments. I could even touch her hand that reaches my way if only my father's arm wasn't so heavy on my shoulders.

I shift under him, try to get away, but he holds on tighter and talks and talks and talks.

"She's with God now," he says.

"It's a boy," Dr. Olsen says, "and he looks great."

I lie back on the bed and reach for my baby at the same time.

"Give him, give him, give him to me," I say.

Dr. Olsen barely has time to wrap him up and she lays him on my chest.

I move my arms around his tiny body, pulling him to be against my heart. He is so small, but he feels sturdy in my arms. He makes this wobbly cry sound.

I laugh and cry, touching his body slick with that white goo that helps him slide safe into this world. There are his arms, his fingers, his chest, his legs, and his toes.

His cry sucks in and then it comes out again, a little stronger, a little louder.

I touch over his face, this perfect heart of a face with eyes as dark as Egyptian stones.

Life and death come through the same door.

He puffs his chest, sucks in another deep breath, and cries so loud this time everyone in the room laughs at the sound of him.

No one has ever looked so beautiful to me.

I press my lips against his head and whisper, "Welcome, baby," except I can't hear myself over the sound of his powerful cry.

# NEVER SAY NEVER

My son hasn't been in my arms for more than ten minutes when a nurse reaches as if he is hers. She wears latex gloves, her hair is stuffed under a shower cap, and her mouth and nose are covered with a mask.

Spencer lies on my chest, his heart against my heart and under my hand, I can feel the whole length of his spine.

He's been in me for all these months, wired into my blood and soul, and now he needs to smell me, to hear my voice, and to be in my arms. That's the way it's supposed to be and I know it from the center of myself. It's one of those core truths about mothers and babies, but the nurse reaches for him just the same.

"We're going to do a couple of tests," she says.

I lift my hand off Spencer's back and let the nurse take him away.

Steve's on a stool next to the bed and he holds my hand and smiles with something like pride, as if he had no idea I was capable of pushing a baby into the world. Dr. Olsen's between my legs on her own stool and she mops at the mess down there. Two other nurses throw bloody towels and used needles into plastic garbage bags. Across the room, the nurse who took Spencer stands at a table and moves over him with fast hands.

"Six pounds, two ounces," she calls out.

"Wow," Steve says, "that seems big for a premature baby, doesn't it?"

Doctor Olsen looks up, the reflection of Steve and me in her safety glasses.

"That is big," she says.

"Nineteen inches long," the nurse says.

"Long too," Steve says.

Doctor Olsen nods and we nod too, and in all of our nodding try to untangle the last week of fear that's been twisted into our gut. Premature babies can be born with all kinds of problems. Premature babies can die.

Past Doctor Olsen, I try to see what's going on with my baby. Spencer's foot goes up in the air for a second and then his hand reaches up too.

"He's an eight," the nurse says, "and a nine."

"Those are the Apgar scores," Doctor Olsen says, "for reflexes and breathing."

"Ten is the best you can get, right?" Steve says.

"That's right," she says.

Steve holds my hand tighter and I swear, he looks a little misty.

"He's fine," Steve says.

"I told you," I say.

He nods and shakes his head at the same time.

"You did," he says. "You were right."

"We need to get a tape recorder," I say. "I want that for the record."

We laugh and he kisses my forehead.

Across the room, the nurse puts a blue-and-pink cap on Spencer's head and lifts him into her arms.

I adjust the covers and get my arms open to take him back.

The nurse moves Spencer closer to her own body and shakes her head.

"We have to take him to the ICU," she says.

I'm all pinned down, my legs spread wide, half of me covered in a hospital gown, the other half of me hanging out all over the place and it's not my power position.

I grab Steve's forearm.

"But he's okay," I say. "His scores are good."

Steve does this powerless shrug that only takes one shoulder.

"We need to perform more tests," the nurse says, "after all, he's still premature."

"But I don't understand," I say, "he's fine, you just said he was fine."

I'm looking at Steve, at Doctor Olsen, at the nurse.

"He is fine," the nurse says, "but it's for his own good, we can't take any chances."

I want to ask what kind of chances she's talking about. I want to ask what could possibly happen between now and ten minutes from now. Past my questions, there's this lion mother in me who wants to roar, the child is mine, give him back to me.

My mouth is so dry, I can't speak.

Steve puts a hand on my shoulder like he knows something and gets off his stool.

"It's fine, Jen," he says, "I'll go with them."

He gets around the obstacle course of machines and IV stands.

"Here," he says, reaching out, "I'll take him."

The nurse isn't quick to give Spencer up, but Steve's not dropping his arms.

The nurse eases the baby over and he's so small between them.

I should be the one holding him.

I push up on my elbows.

"Watch everything," I say.

Steve stops at the door and the nurse behind him stops short too.

"I will," he says.

"Ask questions," I say.

"I will."

"Don't leave him."

"I won't."

I can't go to the ICU, but Steve tells me how it went.

When they got there, Spencer was laid on a rectangle table under bright white lights. Another doctor was there, an expert on premature babies, and he went to work. Steve kept his finger in the center of Spencer's tiny palm while the man pushed needles into his newborn skull and arm. They started IVs for possible infections and gave him saline solution. A nurse taped the IV tubes to Spencer's arm and taped monitors to his chest and back. While all this was going on, Steve asked, "why this, why that," but the nurses and the doctor would only say, "just in case."

"Just in case he develops an infection."

"Just in case he gets dehydrated."

"Just in case his heart stops."

"Just in case he stops breathing."

Spencer cried from the pain of the needles and the tape and the general lack of respect being shown to his new naked self.

Steve leaned down and whispered close to Spencer's ear.

"You're okay, buddy, you're going to be just fine."

The doctor told Steve to move then, he said Steve was in the way.

Steve didn't want to, but he took his finger out of Spencer's small palm and Spencer's fingers closed on his own fist.

Steve took a couple steps back from the table where the doctor and nurses worked and Spencer cried so hard, his face looked like a knot. He couldn't be close to the baby, but he couldn't leave him. All Steve could do was sit in a chair across the room and put his head into his hands.


One day, I found my father in his bedroom and he sat on the edge of their bed with his head in his hands.

His wide back was humped over like a big, sad animal and it was the first time I'd ever seen such a thing. My father hardly ever sat still and when he did, he sure didn't look like someone who might be sad or even crying.

I didn't know how long my mother had been dead. It had been a while, at least a few days, but I wasn't the best with time. Back then, every day was so long from the empty feeling that lay heavy over my bones. My emptiness filled every space of the apartment, every cupboard and closet and room. I'm sure it filled up the clock too and made it move extra slow.

My father said she was with God, that I should be happy for her, and it was this kind of talk that made sad worse. I didn't want God to have my mother. We needed her here. What did He need with her anyway? It wasn't fair and that kind of thinking proved I wasn't just sad, I was angry too. I couldn't be happy. What was wrong with me, anyway?

I was sure I was the only one feeling so mixed up and was doing my best to get through each minute of each day. Sometimes, it took everything just to walk across the room.

When I saw my father sitting so still and sad with his head in his hands, I didn't feel alone anymore and I climbed up on their big California king to be with him.

When my weight moved the bed, my father turned my way.

"What are you doing, Juniper?" he said.

That's the way it was with us. We always called each other names that were different from our real names. I was Jennifer, but he called me Juniper after the song "Jennifer Juniper." He was Joseph, but only strangers called him Joe. Everyone in the family called him Bud.

I knee-walked over to him and the soft of the bed gave in under my weight. I sat down so we were side by side, hip to hip, shoulder to shoulder. I put my arm around his back then, like I was the big person and he was small. My father's back was so wide, I couldn't get my arm all the way around and had to hold his sweater to keep myself that way.

"I miss her," I said.

He nodded on that.

"I do too, Juniper," he said.

I nodded like he nodded and took a deep breath.

"If you wait for me," I said, "I'll marry you."

My father stopped nodding then and all sorts of things happened in his dusty spice eyes. They blinked and shifted around and kept his secrets all at the same time and in there, I saw the shadow of how he didn't believe.

"I mean it," I said, "I'll take care of you and I won't ever get sick."

My father's mouth was one of his best things, it was wide for big smiles and all his white teeth and when he didn't smile, he had these full soft lips. He rolled his lips in while I talked.

He moved a bit of my hair off my face and tucked it behind my ear.

"You are going to grow up to be a beautiful woman," he said, "and you'll fall in love with a wonderful guy who will be a lot better for you than me."

I shook my head so hard, the hair behind my ear came loose.

"I'll never love anyone like you," I said, "never."

My father laughed a little at that, not a real laugh, but a grown-up, I-know-better-than-you laugh. He shifted me on the bed then, pulling me on his lap even though I was almost eight.

"You should never say never, Juniper," he said, "I know about these things."

He snuggled me into that curve of his chest where my ear was up against his heart. His voice vibrated right into my

body while he talked about how he was my father and fathers
weren't the same as husbands and that one day, I'd grow up to
understand.

After a while, I didn't listen anymore, I didn't care what he
said. I knew my own heart and I knew I'd love him forever.
One day, I knew I'd even prove him wrong.

Four days later, on a Monday, Spencer is released from the
hospital.

It's ten in the morning when we get the call that we can
take him home.

Steve and I are in the Intensive Care Unit and all our stuff
is packed up. The car seat is balanced on a table and I lower
Spencer down.

"You got it?" I say.

"I got it," Steve says.

Steve holds all the straps and buckles back and I lay
Spencer in the center of the seat.

Spencer sleeps, which seems impossible as Steve tugs on
his legs and arms.

"Gentle, honey," I say.

"I'm being gentle," Steve says, "I have to get his leg
through this other strap."

"I know," I say, "but you don't have to yank him so hard."

A nurse who just came on her shift is reading our file, trying to catch up on what's been going on.

That's the way it's been over the last four days. Every eight
hours, a new person appears and we have to go over the whole
story of how Spencer is premature but normal and that we are
working to pass all these tests in order to get out of this place.

He had to pass a blood test to show he didn't have an infection.

He had to have a bowel movement to prove he could poop.

He had to breast-feed to prove he could eat.

He had to be tested for jaundice to prove his liver was working right.

He had to be on a heart and lung monitor for forty-eight hours, to prove what? That he was alive?

It felt crazy to me. Later, when I got the bill for twelve thousand dollars, it felt manipulative too, but who was I to argue? I just wanted to go home.

Steve snaps the last buckle into place and we both stand back.

A spiderweb of straps are over Spencer's chest and around his legs.

Steve tilts his head a little and I do it too and then we look at each other like what now?

"Should I prop some blankets around his head?" I say.

"That's a good idea," Steve says, nodding.

I roll blankets up to be thin snakes and prop Spencer's head up to be more comfortable, not that he'd know. The kid is comatose.

Steve and I are wiped out too. Steve's exhaustion is in the gray color of his skin and the lines around his eyes.

"Let's get out of here," I say.

"I agree," Steve says.

The nurse puts her file down then and comes over.

"You did it," she says. "Looks great."

There are a bunch of papers for us to sign and Steve does that while I gather the baby bag, my purse, our coats, and an extra baby blanket.

After Steve's done the nurse closes the file on Spencer and gets a Polaroid camera from behind the counter.

"Let's get a photo," she says.

I shake my head no way, but Steve's game.

"Come on, Jen," he says, "we have to take a picture."

The nurse holds the camera up to her eye and waves her free arm in my general direction.

"Come on, Mom," she says, "get in there."

I don't say no to Steve and the nurse, but I don't put my stuff down either. Instead, I move close to Spencer and paste a smile on my face.

The nurse presses the button and the flash is bright in my eyes. The photo spits from a slot in front of the camera.

"Let's see if it's a good one," the nurse says.

She waves the square of the picture in the air and there's that beat of time where we all stand around and wait for the image to take form.

"You guys sure made a pretty baby," the nurse says. "Is he your first?"

"Yes," Steve says, "he is."

"I remember my first," the nurse says, her face gone dreamy. "He was so sweet, I ended up having two more."

"Wow," Steve says.

I shift from one foot to the other, itching to get out the door, but nod with the conversation, as if I'm actually paying attention.

"Can you imaging having another one, Jen?" Steve says.

"What?" I say.

Steve's face is all good-natured, the way he gets when chatting about nothing.

"Another baby?" he says.

I laugh but it's not a happy sound, it's this choke out of me.

"Absolutely not," I say, "I am never having another baby."

The nurse nods the nod of a sage.

"Never say never," she says.

She slides the half-developed photo on the counter and it comes into focus in front of our eyes to be Steve and me with the tiny loaf of Spencer buckled into his massive car seat.

I can barely take in the three of us in the photograph and have no idea what the next hour is going to be like. It's fair to say I will never have another baby because right now, it's true. I'd never willingly go through this whole thing again.

The photo seems to be overdeveloping, the colors bleeding brighter in the picture than they are in real life.

Steve takes up the suitcase that's next to the door and reaches for the car seat.

"Ready?" Steve says.

I take the photo off the counter and slip it into the pocket of my bag.

"You bet," I say, "let's go."


In Santa Monica there is a restaurant built at the end of a long wooden pier that runs down the beach and over the ocean.

About three months after my mother died, my father and I went there for dinner. It was this special night out with just the two of us, a grown-up dinner with candles, tablecloths, and people who lifted glasses of wine.

He picked a table at the far end of the restaurant, and out the window was the ocean. If you opened the window, you could fall right in.

I didn't like the ocean, it was too vast and deep, but my father loved and longed for it in the way grown-ups love and long for things.

Sitting there, I could feel the power of the water through the floor and into my legs, but I made myself be still. My father was my ocean.

He was getting married to another woman I didn't like, but I told myself it didn't matter; when I grew up, he'd see she was wrong for him. The woman was pretty, but she had no sense of style and she wasn't nice to him at all.

On his side of the table, he was talking to the waitress about the menu. She kept calling him Joe since he made the reservation for us under his first name, Joseph, but finally he said she could just call him Bud. She smiled when he said that and blushed up to her ears. That's the way it was with my dad. He made girls blush, he was that handsome, he was that charming.

While he talked and the waitress blushed, I was on my side of the table doing the math on how I'd be eighteen in about ten years and how ten years would go by pretty fast.

Finally, he gave the waitress his menu and smiled his charm my way.

I smiled back and tried to think of something smart and funny to say, but he didn't wait. He was off in his mind the way he always was, looking out the window and then he squinted.

"Look at that," he said.

I leaned my elbows on the table and balanced on the edge of my chair.

The sun was reflected on the calm ocean that was shined deep blue. The sky was a buttery pink and there were a few lazy clouds pulled flat and lying still.

His finger pressed to the glass of the window. "Do you see it?" he said.

Out a ways there was one gray cloud that poured down a circle of storm. Below the cloud, the ocean was broken up by hard raindrops, and in that part of the water no sun could shine.

"What is it?" I said.

My father curled his finger back into his hand and his eyebrows went high on his forehead.

"It's rain, silly," he said.

I sat back in my chair and looked at both his eyes, like looking deep into his head that knew everything.

"I know," I said, "but why? Why is it there and why now when there's no other clouds?"

My father's dusty spice eyes went wide with my questions and his mouth was shaped up to laugh at me.

"I don't know why," he said, "just because, I guess."

"There's got to be a reason," I said, "there's got to be some science about it or maybe it's like God sending a message."

My father put his hands together and rested his chin on his fingers, speaking very slow, like I was stupid or something.

"Some things don't have a reason, Juniper," he said, "they happen just because."

I watched him for a long time, but I could tell he really didn't know why and he was using "just because" as an excuse. There was a reason for everything, you just had to dig to find it.

Our drinks came then, red wine for him, a glass of soda for me. He lifted his glass in my direction. I took up my glass too, bubbles in the clear soda jumping around the ice, and I touched his glass so careful.

"Here's to my girl," he said.

*          *          *

It's mid-July and summer wind blows through the tops of the pines and maples and the air is soft with the promise of long hot days.

Spencer holds the chains of his swing tight and tilts his head back.

"Under doggy," he says.

"Okay," I say.

I push against his back, one swing, two swings, and on the third swing I push hard and run at the same time. Spencer laughs, his feet up to the sun and then he comes back to swing just as high the other way.

A little boy and his father are in the swing next to us, but the man is lost in his own thoughts.

I put my face to the sun and close my eyes. Inside my head, it's quiet in a way it hasn't been since Spencer was born.

He's three years old now and out of diapers, he sleeps through the night, he can talk in complete sentences, and I don't have to follow his every move in this kind of deathly fear that he's going to kill himself if he takes three steps away from me.

We're at this place where I can actually hear myself think, except I'm not thinking. I'm just being quiet and I like the way the sun feels on my skin.

"Let's go, Dad," the little boy says and when I open my eyes, he's gone from the other swing and running down the hill of grass, his father a few steps behind.

I catch the chains of Spencer's swing and pull him back to me.

"Do you want to keep swinging?" I say, "or do you want to go now?"

"Keep swinging," Spencer says.

"Okeydokey," I say.

I pull the swing all the way back and let him go again.

On the sidewalk, brittle leaves move in an undercurrent of wind and they turn on themselves with that crisp sound of fall, even though fall is two months away.

Just when you settle into one season, another one is coming faster than you think.

The empty swing next to Spencer moves just a little and I watch it like a meditation, pushing Spencer every time he swings back in my direction.

In the space of nothing in the empty swing, I see a child of mine who I would call Joe. "Hey Spencer, hey Joe," I can hear my own voice say out the back door and into the afternoon of another time. I can hear myself calling, "Come in, kids, it's time for dinner." I can hear myself laugh and say, "Yeah, those are my boys, Spencer and Joe."

Spencer's voice calls for me then, his real-time voice. His feet drag in the bark chips and his swing has stopped.

"Push, Mommy," Spencer says, "you're not pushing."

A year after we had our dinner in Santa Monica, my father had a heart attack.

It happened as we passed Thanksgiving and were on the way to December, the month that cupped in its hand the biggest days of the year, my birthday and Christmas. December now held my father's life.

I couldn't go to the hospital, but my stepmother could and she took her oldest with her. When the two of them came home, they would talk about how he had machines hooked up to his arms and tubes up his nose.

On the first day, they said he looked so bad they thought he was dead.

On the second, they said he looked a little better and that his skin wasn't so gray.

On the third day, they said he looked so good he was coming home.

On the fourth day, he died. They were taking a tube out of his throat and he had another heart attack. Everyone was so surprised. My stepmother said there wasn't a real reason, it just happened.

He died on a Saturday night in December and birthdays and Christmas didn't matter. There was no mother and no father. There was no one to marry one day and no one to prove wrong.

It's a year after that day in the park and Spencer is four years old. He's off at pre-school. I curl up on the bench seat of our kitchen nook with the newspaper and a cup of coffee. In the horoscope section, mine reads: "Inheritances come from a distant relative, stay close to the telephone."

Steve's in another part of the house and he talks loud the way he does when he's on the telephone, as if the other person on the line is deaf. By the time he hits the kitchen, his voice is so loud, I can't concentrate on the stars.

I used to do this hand motion that said, "Take it down a notch, Sport," and would verbalize the same in the form of advice after he hung up, but after years of having both hand motions and advice ignored, I was down to staring at Steve in a kind of irritated disbelief that he never seemed to notice.

"THANK YOU," Steve yells.

He pushes the off button on the remote and puts the hand-set on the kitchen counter.

"June twentieth," he says. "It's all set."

I fold the newspaper in half and toss it on the table.

"Are you going to do it this time?" I say.

Steve nods extra times to prove sincerity.

"You bet, Baby," he says, "it's as good as done."

Steve works his fingers like the blades of a pair of scissors, hacking at the air between us.

"Snip, snip," he says, "clip, clip."

"Oh Steve, honestly," I say. "Do you have to be so graphic?"

Steve grins to show all his pretty white teeth and slides into his side of the booth. He takes the coffee pot and pours a little more into his own cup.

"Are you sure you want me to go through with it?" he says. "Are you sure you don't want a cute little girl?"

He lifts the pot in my direction.

I put my hand over my coffee mug.

"No more," I say. "No more coffee and no more kids."

Steve shrugs like it's my loss and puts the pot down again. He picks up his part of the paper, the section on the stock market with its columns of teeny-tiny numbers, and puts a pair of glasses on his face.

"Why would you ask me that?"

Steve lets a corner of the paper fall down and his glasses are low on his nose.

"What?" he says.

"Why would you ask if I want a little girl?" I say.

Steve frowns a little and shrugs just one shoulder.

"I don't know," he says, "just because, I guess."

I rearrange myself in the booth to cross my legs under the table and sit up straight.

"No, no, no," I say, "not just because. We've talked about this thing. I thought we decided we didn't want more kids."

Steve lets the paper down all the way and takes off his glasses.

"I'm fine with whatever we do," he says, "but I've said it before and I'll say it now, I'm leaving this one up to you, Jen."

He holds his glasses while he talks, waving them in the air between us.

"You probably could use another baby," he says.

There is a tired feeling inside of me that comes when we talk about another baby. It's like being on an endless circle where I just don't have an answer.

I lean elbows on the table and put my face into my hands. Over Steve's shoulder is a window with a view of a bird feeder. Little gray birds perch in there, poking at the seed we laid out.

I love Spencer, I love him more than I can stand. In fact, I love him as much as I loved my own father and mother and that's a hard love to have, especially when you know it can disappear in a heartbeat. It's this bald, crazy, impossible love that is just killing me. I just don't think I have it in me to be that open, to be that afraid and, God, what if something went wrong with the next baby? How could I live?

"So?" Steve says, "what do you want to do?"

The birds fight in the feeder and then they all lift up and fly away.

I let out a deep breath and sit back in the booth with this heavy weight of indecision and I shake my head.

"I don't know, Steve," I say, "I really don't know."

It's the first week of June and I'm in the bathroom trying to figure out how to take a pregnancy test.

Spencer's at school again and Steve's on the road between Portland and Seattle.

The instructions on the box say I'm supposed to pee on this small slip of a stick and into this even smaller rectangle of a window. If I aim right, one line will mean I'm not pregnant and two will mean I am. They are very simple instructions, but they keep falling out of my head. I have to read them over and over again.

It's impossible to do it without peeing all over my hand, but I finally hit the rectangle.

I put the stick on the edge of the sink and wash my hands.

In the sound of the running water, I'm all chatty in my head about how silly this is, how I've never made a mistake and now there is no way I am pregnant.

I turn the water off, dry my hands on a towel, and the lines come into focus. There is the one, a thick blue line, and then there is another one that lifts just above it.

One means no? Two means yes? Or is it one means yes and two means no. I grab the instructions off the shelf.

Two lines means you are having a baby.

I pick up the stick and hold it closer to my face, yes, those are two lines.

I put the stick down and burst into tears.

I sit on the toilet and put my hands over my face, crying the way you do when you've made a decision in spite of yourself.

I pull tissues and blow my nose.

Leaving the stick in the bathroom, I go to find the telephone. I dial Steve's cell phone number and while it rings, dig into my purse for my date book.

"HELLO," Steve yells.

"Steve?" I say.

"HEY, JEN," Steve yells. "WHAT ARE YOU DOING?"

I pull the date book out and drop my purse, flipping open the book to the month of May.

"Steve," I say, "you don't have to talk so loud."

"Sorry," he says.

I move the telephone to my other ear.

"Honey," I say, "I've got some news."

It's quiet on the line and Steve clears his throat.

"You're pregnant?" he says.

I let out my breath.

"How did you know that?" I say.

"I had a feeling," he says.

It's quiet on the line and I can hear the sounds of his car through the telephone. I wish I could see his face, I wish I could see if he was mad or happy.

"I've got the vasectomy thing next week," he finally says.

"I know," I say.

"Are you crying?" he says.

I nod even though he can't see that.

"Are you happy or are you sad?" he says.

I shake my head and move the tears to spill off the edge of my fingers.

"I just can't understand how we made that kind of mistake," I say.

Steve laughs at that.

"Some things don't make sense, Jen," Steve says. "Besides, I thought you needed another baby."

I know he's right about needing another baby; I may not want one, but I probably need one. I don't agree that this doesn't make sense though.

I move my hand over my date book and find the place where the months lay out for the whole year. I count from the time this would have happened, a couple weeks ago, to when the baby will be here in forty weeks.

"You okay?" Steve says.

"Yeah," I say.

I wipe my nose with the back of my arm and the tears are gone with the focus of counting.

"I'm looking to see when this baby will come."

Steve is quiet and my count stops in the first week of February.

"February," I say.

"You're kidding," he says.

"Nope," I say, "if my count is right, we are looking at a baby coming on my father's birthday, or darn close to it."

Steve is quiet and between us, there is a spark in the air that is something like awe.

I start to cry again, I can't help it, it's like my father is on the other side of those numbers in the date book, it's like he's been there all along, nudging at my shoulder and saying, "Never say never, Juniper," without saying a word.

"I guess we're calling this baby Joe," Steve says.

I laugh out loud and nod, even though I know he can't see me.

"And if it's a girl," I say, "let's call her Josephine."

## BROTHERS AND SISTERS

I hold the covers back and Spencer wiggles his legs between his airplane sheets. His shins are bruised from climbing trees and he has a glow-in-the-dark Band-Aid wrapped around his toe, not because he's hurt, he just loves Band-Aids.

"What's it going to be tonight?" I say, "*All About Fire Trucks* or *Green Eggs and Ham?*"

Spencer pulls his covers up around his body and gets his bear on his lap.

"Trucks," Spencer says.

I pull *All About Fire Trucks* off his bookshelf and toss it on the end of his bed.

Every other night, bedtime with Spencer is my job. I give him a shower, blow his hair dry with the hair dryer, and help him brush and floss his teeth. He hugs Steve and then we go up to his room where he picks a book.

Steve likes sitting in a chair next to Spencer's bed when he reads, but when it's my turn, I like to lie on the bed and snuggle against him.

I shift to get all the way on his narrow bed.

"You have to move over a little," I say.

Spencer moves himself and Bear over a little, but not enough, and he pushes his elbow into my stomach.

"There's no more room," he says. "You're too fat."

"It's not me," I say, "it's the baby."

Spencer eyes my stomach and we've talked about her a little bit, mostly at bedtime like this, while we're getting comfortable. I've told him that it's a girl and that she's getting big enough inside of me to hear our voices while we talk.

We shift and twist a little more, his bed moving under my weight, and finally we are face to face, stomach to stomach, knee to knee. This close, Spencer smells like baby shampoo and toothpaste.

"You know," I say, "she's coming pretty soon and when she gets here, she's going to look up to you."

Spencer is serious the way he gets when he pays attention. He moves his lips in like he's tasting something.

"What's 'look up' mean?" he says.

"It means admire," I say. "Appreciate. Respect. Like."

I move down all the words I can think of and land at the one that's four-year-old friendly. I nod my head on "like."

"That's it," I say, "she's going to like you a lot."

"Why?" Spencer says.

I lift my shoulder up and let it fall in a quick shrug.

"That's just the way it is," I say. "It's what little sisters do."

Spencer is so rarely still and when he is, I can't help but touch him.

I trace the small bones of his cheeks and jaw. It always gets me how fragile he is.

I take my hand off Spencer and push it between my knees, my elbows pushing into my baby-full stomach.

"When she gets here, you have to be really nice to her," I say, "can you do that for me?"

Spencer nods like, "Sure, of course."

"I mean it, Spencer," I say, "you're going to be so much bigger than her and you have to try extra hard to be sweet."

Spencer rolls away and reaches to something on the floor.

"Do you understand what I am trying to say?"

Spencer rolls back and points a flashlight direct in my face.

"I can see up your nose," he says.

I put my whole hand over the light.

"Please don't do that," I say.

Spencer yanks the light away and shines it into my face again.

It's this game we have. He shines the light into my eyes and I make a very serious face and say, "Don't shine that light into my eyes. You're making me go blind."

The whole thing is hilarious to him and he laughs like I'm some kind of stand-up comedian.

I put my hand over the light this time and shake my head.

"Not now," I say, "I want you to tell me that you understand what I'm saying."

Spencer's done listening though. He points the light at the ceiling and moves it around up there. He draws over the edge of the big circle of blue sky I painted up there. There are clouds in his sky and I even put a little black airplane in the clouds.

They say a sibling changes everything. Once the second baby arrives, your oldest feels his first murderous instinct and I can vouch for that. The way I remember it, my brother tried to take me out at least two times before I was three. Once, he got me to the top of our carport and shoved me off. "I thought she could fly," B.J. said. Another time, he pulled open a gate and let a big dog into our yard. That dog took a huge bite out of my face. It wasn't attempted murder, but I knew he didn't like me very much.

Spencer moves his light to the letters of the alphabet that snake A to Z over his walls and then over the shelves that hold all his books and toys. He turns the light on his own face.

"Can you see up my nose?" he says.

His nostrils are lit-up black holes.

"Yeah," I say, "and I can see all your boogers too."

I move my hands down his sides and wiggle fingers into his soft spots.

"That's so gross," I say.

Spencer giggles and puts the light in my face, giving me a second chance.

I make my serious face.

"Don't shine that light into my eyes," I say, "you're making me go blind."

Spencer laughs so hard he falls off the bed.

When I was nine years old, we lived in Palo Alto in a rented house on a hill. There was B.J., me, our stepmother, and her three kids. By that time B.J. didn't like to be called B.J., he just wanted to be called Bryan. Each one of us kids had a separate room and the house was so big, I could be at one end and not hear anything going on at the other.

My room was the one painted pink with the white canopy bed and furniture to match. I kept it all picked up and had all my toys and books arranged on the shelves.

One night, I was lying in my bed with a stuffed lamb and a pair of hugging hippos tight against my heart.

My room was dark but not dark, moonlight making shadows through the pink curtains that matched the pink bedspread.

The house was quiet but I couldn't sleep.

Every time I tried, my bed moved with a shiver feeling, like something big was under the mattress.

That day we went to the movies, all five of us kids and a baby-sitter, who thought it would be fun to see *The Exorcist*.

"It's your Easter treat," he said, laughing like he had made a joke.

Our stepmother was in Los Angeles doing some kind of business and the baby-sitter, this small guy with a strange laugh, was staying at the house.

I couldn't watch the whole movie, it scared me that bad, and I ended up in another theater playing *The Sting*. I leaned against the back wall of the theater and made myself not think about the possessed girl whose hair was a mess.

With ragtime music, Robert Redford, and Paul Newman it was easy to let the devil slip out of my head. When the lights were out and I was in my own bed that night, the devil was there though, waiting in the shadows. I didn't know what he looked like, but I could feel him. He was a thick, heavy, hot-blanket feeling, and if I closed my eyes for one minute or took another breath he would rush up like steam, push down my throat, and take over my soul.

My mouth was dry of spit and I shifted to the edge of the bed. I put one leg over the end, but thought better of it. If I stepped down, the devil might grab my ankle and suck me under.

I put my stuffed animals down and stood up instead. I steadied myself against the soft roll of the mattress, dipped so I didn't hit my head on the canopy, and jumped long, the feel of the floor through my feet and into my whole body.

With the devil at the back of my bare legs, I ran out of my room, around the love seat in the family room, and to the closed door with the GO AWAY sign taped on.

Only the devil at my back would make me break Bryan's rule about going in without knocking first. My legs tingled and I turned his knob real slow. His drapes were pulled closed and I stood extra still, waiting for my eyes to get right with the dark.

Bryan had to be awake. Who could really sleep after *The Exorcist?* I could hear his raspy breathing sound that was almost a snore and when the dark unfolded to show form, I could see him on his back in his bed.

I went over, kneeled down, and this close to Bryan, it felt like the devil was pulling back.

I couldn't really see Bryan's face but I didn't need to. I knew him like I knew myself. We had the same dark hair, dark eyes, and smooth tan skin. The difference between us was that he was a few shades darker than me, his eyes and hair were almost black.

"Bryan," I whispered.

His breathing changed and he made tasting sounds with his mouth.

"Bryan," I whispered again.

He moved in his bed, rolling from his back to his side.

"Jenny?"

"Yeah," I whispered.

I put my hand on the cool of his sheets, reaching for him but knowing that I couldn't touch.

There was a rule between Bryan and me, this rule that came after our mom died and our father married the stepmother. It wasn't my rule, it was Bryan's rule and it wasn't said out loud, it just was. The rule was he didn't talk to me and never wanted me to touch him. Now that Dad had died too, the rule didn't seem fair. With the way things were in Palo Alto with the stepmother and her kids and now this baby-sitter, Bryan and I together were all I had left in the world. I just wanted to be with him, at least next to each other on the sofa at TV time, at the dining-room table during dinner, or in the car when we went places, but Bryan didn't want any of that. He wanted me on the other side of his GO AWAY sign. I moved my hand on the cool of his sheets.

"What are you doing in here?" he said.

His voice sounded like he used to sound before our mother died, before he made everyone stop calling him B.J., before the rule.

"I think the devil is under my bed," I said.

It got quiet between us and he was thinking about it. I wondered what would come next but I was too scared to even guess. I couldn't go back to my own room and I knew he wouldn't let me come under his covers.

"You can sleep on the floor," he said finally.

"Really?"

He moved around then and there was a tug and pull sound and something dropped on the floor.

"Use this," he said.

It was a blanket and then something else fell.

"You can have my pillow too," he said.

I caught the pillow that was warm from his head. The smell of him was there, toothpaste, clean hair, and something else too.

I felt the tingle feeling around my eyes, but Bryan hated it when I cried. I pushed my face into his pillow, pushed in hard, and when I knew I wouldn't sound like I was crying, I came up for air.

"Thanks," I said.

Bryan didn't say anything. He shifted in his own bed and turned his back on me.

I moved around on the floor, getting myself comfortable, and wrapped the blanket around from shoulder to toes. The carpet was scratchy through my thin nightgown but I didn't care. I was there with my brother, I was safe, and I knew the devil wasn't going to get my soul, at least, not that night.


It's more than a month after Spencer and I talked about what kind of big brother he was going to be and we're on the way to school.

He's back in his car seat and I'm up front. My stomach is so far ahead of me, I can't drive without moving my seat all the way back.

" 'Obladee,' " Spencer says.

I adjust the rearview to see him.

"Over and over or just once?"

"Over and over," he says.

I push the buttons on the CD player until I get to his music request. I press the repeat button so it's the only song we'll hear and the music takes over.

Ahead of us, a school bus stops, red lights flashing. The driver unfolds a stop sign. On the back of the bus, there is another sign that says it's unlawful to pass a bus that has its flashing lights on.

I slow down and stop.

Parents stand on the sidewalk, waving good-bye, and their kids climb on the bus single file.

It's *Ob-La-Di Ob-La-Da, life goes on, bra, La-la-la how the life goes on.* Spencer sings with the words, his head rocking side to side.

I've never talked to Spencer about Bryan. Where are the four-year-old-friendly words to say that we were separated when I was eleven and Bryan was thirteen, that I only saw him three more times in my life, and that he shot himself in the head when he was just twenty-three?

I'm thirty-eight and I still don't have the right words to explain it all to myself. I like to think I'm over all that happened with Bryan, but now I have Spencer and I'm about to have a little girl, I think about the idea of brothers and sisters all the time.

There is one truth I know. Even when I'm not thinking about Bryan, I am thinking about him. I want to understand why he was so angry, so mean, and so untouchable for me. I want to understand the rule and how he had to make his heart so hard and why, in spite of everything, I still loved him so much. I want to understand why he killed himself and, most of all, I want to know he didn't do it because of anything to do with me. I want to know that when he grew up and looked back, he didn't see his own failure as a big brother and let that be one of his reasons to die.

When I figure it all out, that's when I can really say the right things about brothers and sisters to Spencer. Right now, I don't have a clue.

The bus driver pulls the stop sign in and turns off the lights. Boys and girls are in the bus, faces close to the windows. A boy makes a funny face and a couple of girls wave.

I smile at the boy and wave at the girls.

Spencer says something I can't hear and I turn the music down.

"What, honey?" I say.

"Andy is a good big brother," he says.

I look at Spencer in the rearview.

"What?" I say.

"Andy is a good big brother," he says.

The bus stops at the next intersection and its blinker signals a right turn.

"Is Andy a kid in your class?"

Spencer puts his hands out, palms up.

"Mom," Spencer says. "You know, *ANDY*."

The bus turns and it's my turn at the sign. I pull forward and wait for the right of way.

I turn around to look at Spencer head-on and he wears his big green coat with a hood pulled up over his head. His face under the hood is so small and pale and his dark eyes are full of his own thoughts.

Andy, Andy, who the hell is Andy, but then, I get it.

"*Toy Story?*" I say.

Spencer nods like, "Duh, finally."

"Okay," I say, "I'm with you."

I pull through the intersection and there is no more traffic in front of me. It's a clear shot through the neighborhood.

"And Sid is a bad big brother," Spencer says.

"That's right," I say, "he hurt his sister, didn't he?"

Spencer nods and his face is so serious under his hood. He looks out the window again and I drive around the bend where it's a neighborhood of old house after old house. The trees are old too and they are deep in winter sleep, full of bare branches that tangle to the sky.

It's a miracle to watch Spencer translate our talk a month ago into the language of a movie with a message he can understand. Right now, he's working the idea of right and wrong in his own mind and balancing it against the things I said about his little sister and the things I didn't say about my own brother. He's making all the connections in his head and putting a story together about a future where things will be expected of him. But I wonder, is it too much? Is this how it started for Bryan?

The music is low, but it's still there, *la-la-la*.

Spencer looks at me in the rearview.

"I'm going to be like Andy," he says.

I slow the car down for the stop sign and put my hand between the seats, reaching back to him.

I say, "You're a great kid, Spence."

Spencer nods like he knows this already at least, I hope he does. He puts his small hand into mine and it's hard to drive with my arm back that way, but I don't care. I keep a hold of him for the rest of the drive, holding hands and listening to the music about how life seems to go on and on.

# LINKS

Three A.M. shadows come through the slats of the window blind. Out the window, streetlights shine amber circles on the wet and empty street. A row of maples are bare of leaves and their branches reach high like old women's skinny arms with so many questions.

I hold Josephine and her baby weight molds into the deflated soft of my stomach.

In our room, there is a narrow bed with metal railings to keep us from falling, a side table on wheels that holds a box of tissues, and a water bottle that has the words "Providence Hospital" printed on clear plastic. Across the room, there is the shape of the television suspended from the ceiling and against the wall, more shapes of the sofa, a chair, a round table, and two more chairs. Other than Josephine, me, and the teddy bear that Spencer sent to get us safely through our first night, we are alone with the furniture and the shadows.

An hour ago, we weren't alone. An hour ago this room was full of people and light.

An hour ago, Josephine was being born, more and more of her emerging each time I grabbed my breath and pushed. Steve lifted my leg, his way of helping. He said he couldn't believe I was so strong.

Our strength is also our weakness.

The big muscles of my legs were powerful, but the subtle muscles, the ones the Indians call the *bondas*, were small and weak. In bringing my baby through my body, I had to learn to channel power from my legs to those other places and each time I got it wrong, Josephine retreated and I had to try again. It took a long time.

A nurse named Jill stood nearby, giving instructions on how to hold my breath and count inside my head. The doctor named Alice sat in an easy chair with her legs crossed, so casual, so relaxed.

"You're doing great," Alice said. "Don't rush, take your time."

When I got it all right, the breathing, the pushing, the shifting of power within, Josephine finally emerged through the ring of fire, a soft, sticky white baby.

Jill and Alice and Steve and I cried and laughed and looked at one another.

"Oh my God, it's amazing, isn't it?"

Real miracles have a way of stealing verbal eloquence.

In that speechless space, Josephine was given over to me and laid on top of my chest. She was so sturdy and strong and I folded her into myself, as perfect a fit on the outside as she had been on the inside.

For a while, there was the fussing around that goes with a new baby, the weighing and the measuring and the testing for reflexes. When Josephine wasn't with me, she cried and as soon as she was back in the solid fit of my arms, she stopped.

Then Alice left to deliver twins.

Jill said good-bye too. It was the end of her shift.

Steve went home to get some sleep.

The room cleared of people and sound, the light was turned off, and the door swung to a close.

I could have gone to sleep, my body certainly needed the rest. Josephine had already gone to a place that only babies seem to go, two fingers in her mouth as she nodded her chin against her chest

I couldn't sleep though, I had this feeling of a visitor in the shadows. It was this woman who came to call on me, this woman who needed to talk. She said now that Josephine was here and sleeping against my heart, it was time to take a trip with her to the other side.

I once had a friend named Patty. She was small with a wide smile on a moon-round face. Her last name should have been Pie, she was that cute. We lived across the hall from each other, twenty-year-old girls in their first apartments. There was a familiar quality to Patty. It was there in the lost look of her round soft eyes and, after we talked for a while, I found out what the familiar thing was. She had been adopted when she was born, just like me.

We were sitting on the stoop of our apartments, drinking longneck beers without anywhere to go.

Once the adopted thing was out there, we were like best friends.

"Did your real mother get to hold you?" Patty said.

I took a swig of my beer and shook my head.

"I don't think so," I said.

"How do you know?" she said.

"Someone told me I got taken to the nursery right away. Then my parents, Bud and Janet, got me three days later," I said. "How about you?"

Patty leaned with her elbows on her knees and she held her beer by the neck, letting it swing back and forth. She had a far-off look in her eyes.

"I think she held me," Patty said.

I looked in the direction Patty looked, but over there it was just more apartments like ours, a street, and a few trees.

"How do you know?" I said.

Patty turned to me and smiled this secret smile.

"I just know," she said, "I can feel it in my body."

I watched her for such a long time. I had no idea what she meant by that and I tried to feel into my own body for that kind of thing. In me was a kind of emptiness that, if you looked at it long enough, would turn into tears. I drank down the rest of my beer.

Patty wasn't on her own and living across the hall from me for very long before she told me that she had to find her first mother. Her second mother was a good woman, Patty loved her with almost all her heart, but something was missing.

Patty's talk of her first mother couldn't make its way past my ears and into my heart. I couldn't understand it. I couldn't feel it. Thinking about it just made me mad. Adoption was the ultimate rejection. My first mother didn't want me and to make that okay, I wouldn't let myself want to know anything about her.

Patty made calls and was told to write a letter. There was a file in a drawer at the agency and in that file another letter was waiting. The letters fit together to make a whole and just like that, Patty found her real mother. Right away, they were reunited, a family of Patty Pies, small people with wide smiles on moon-round faces. They were cute and happy and their story went like this:

Patty's mother was a teenager and her parents sent her to a place where girls give up their babies. It was a Catholic girls' school in Spokane. Patty's mother had Patty and the nuns let her hold her baby for a whole night. Patty's mom loved her too much to give her up, but she had no money and nowhere to go. In the morning, a nun took Patty away and Patty's mom went back to her life as a daughter living on a farm. Two years later, Patty's mom married Patty's dad and made a family beyond Patty, always longing for her though, always wanting her back.

Way back when I was about eleven years old, I was sent to live with my aunt after Janet and then Bud died. There were a bunch of legal papers that came with me, stuff about my Social Security benefits and life insurance and other things my aunt didn't let me see. She did give me a small rectangle of paper though. It wasn't a whole sheet, it was just half a page and it had a raised seal that read "The State of Nevada." In the lines under the seal, there were typewriter words that put together the details of my first mother and my first father.

I took that page and folded it in half, then in half again, and then in half one more time and slid it between the pages of a

Collier's encyclopedia that I kept on my desk. I'd unfold that paper and memorize the lines of how my first mother was small boned and French and how my first father had dark eyes and dark skin. The lines on that piece of paper held the promise of something familiar, if only in features, and they gave tastes of comfort that come from the idea of family. I liked to close my eyes and imagine people out there who looked like me, who were maybe looking for me too.

After I grew up and moved out of my aunt and uncle's house, I stopped looking at that piece of paper. I kept it stored in the encyclopedia and kept the encyclopedia locked in my trunk, but Patty's reunion with her mother teased me to dig it out and make a telephone call.

A nice woman in Nevada explained the procedure. I write a letter, they open a file, and if my first mother or my first father wrote a letter too, our letters would make a match.

"Then we'll call you and make arrangements," she said, very professional, very polite.

I thought about it for such a long time, my heart like a small child begging candy from a grown-up. Just write, what can it hurt to write? Of course my mother is waiting for me. Who knows how many years her letter has been waiting in a dusty file. Just write. Just write.

I wrote the letter and I waited. I waited and I waited. While I waited, I checked the telephone for a dial tone, I looked at it whenever I walked by, and when I couldn't wait another day, I called.

"Yes," the woman said, very professional, very polite, "we received your letter but no, there are no other letters here yet. We'll call you."

*          *          *

I don't keep in touch with Patty anymore. She has her family now.

I don't have that half sheet of paper either, it got lost in all the times I've moved.

I have called the state of Nevada three times to tell them when I've changed my address. I made those calls from Montana, then Washington, and finally Oregon and they were like whispers of hope crossing state lines from where I was to where my first mother might be waiting. But she never was.

Perhaps she is dead.

Perhaps she forgot.

Perhaps she never wants to remember.

I gave up thinking about her at all. You can't live your life staring at the telephone.

But with Josephine in my arms, her strong new heartbeat against my own, not so strong and not so new anymore, the whispers in the shadows prove that sometimes you think you've given up but you haven't, not really. How could I forget the woman who brought me into the world? How could I not think about her on days like my birthday or on a day like this, when I hold my brand-new daughter in my arms?

In the way that you can only imagine at 3:00 A.M., I let myself fall into the possibility of my first mother. Our story went like this:

My birth had been complicated. Forceps pulled me from her and when it was over, I was wrapped up and taken away. Patty's mom held her all night long, but my mother didn't get her baby. That's the way it was done in Nevada.

When Spencer was born premature, he was taken away from me so the doctors could perform a bunch of tests in a place that I couldn't get to for a few hours. Not being able to have him in my arms shredded my heart down to its core.

I could feel the emptiness of my own mother's arms on the night I was born, and if I could feel all that and see to the past, could I go one more step? Could I send a message over the waves of time between now and then, could I say, "I have a daughter now, she's here and she's beautiful and in holding her I am healing all of us at least a little bit."

Dawn dissolves the dark and the clock rounds past five, but I am still between now and then and my message flows out to my real mother, wherever she was. Perhaps she would get it in a dream and wake up to the memory of me, that daughter she never held but never forgot, or that daughter she did forget until the dream woke her up. Perhaps she was dead but her soul wandered days and nights, in search of answers that only time could give until, finally, she got one more that she could add to her collection before traveling on to other spirit places.

By six, the dark is gone and it's raining. The silence on the empty street has been sliced away by the spray of tires, cars full of people going to work and school and wherever else they need to go. One woman walks under the bare maple trees, her head hidden under the curve of her wide black umbrella.

Josephine stirs against me and takes a deep breath into her nose. She opens her eyes long enough to see me still awake, still watching her, and nods as if to say, "Yes, you're still here." She closes her eyes again, going back to rest and recover and rebuild after her long journey.

The shadows are gone. It is a new day. I close my eyes and sleep moves over me right away. I didn't realize I was so tired.

# NAKED TREES

The day is golden with the glow of red leaves, yellow leaves, orange leaves, leaves, leaves, and still more leaves. They blow off oak trees, chestnut trees, and Japanese maple trees and mix together on the sidewalks and in the gutters.

When it was just me, I used to talk to myself about the trees, this rambling line of conversation in my head about their dispositions. In the spring, there were the trees that came out with leaves right away, even when the nights were still frosty. They were the optimists, those brave and eager souls who didn't care if it was warm or not. They wanted out. Then there were other trees that didn't show leaves for such a long time, their naked branches holding out for warmer winds. They were the pessimists or maybe the deep sleepers or maybe just the ones who were cautious and safe.

When fall came, it was the same thing again. The trees who couldn't wait to dump all their leaves at once were arbor exhibitionists, while others that held on until bitter winds forced their leaves away were the late-night partiers who refused to go home.

The sun shines down on Spencer's hair and I move my hand over the top of his head.

"See the trees that don't have any leaves left?" I say.

Spencer looks ahead, chin up.

"Yeah," he says.

"They're naked," I whisper.

I tip my head side to side and make my voice deep and different.

"Look at me, I'm naked," I say, "I'm a naked tree."

Spencer grins into the corners of his eyes. From farts to burps, he's into all that body stuff, and most of all, he loves naked talk.

"And those trees," I say, pointing to two golden maples, "they're not ready for naked time yet."

"They're shy," he says.

"You think?" I say.

He nods, brown eyes searching ahead, and the rest of the walk is dedicated to flushing out which trees are naked and which ones aren't.

The downtown library is this beauty of dark woods and stone. The inside is like a church, with great arches and cathedral ceilings and a rise of marble steps.

I hold one of the double doors for Spencer and he runs in, coat half-down his arms and shoulders as he goes.

The main gallery is a rush of people in lines and at the computers. People have piles of books they return or want to check out and others stand in line at the information desk.

Spencer zigzags between people and starts up the steps.

I jog to keep up with him, calling, "Slow down," and "Hold the rail," since the marble stairs are as lovely as the rest of this place, but they make you trip. It's the riser, it's not quite right. Maybe the steps were built at a time when people didn't take big steps or maybe there wasn't enough marble to do the job right. Whatever happened, the steps are shorter than regular ones and they hit your body wrong.

Spencer's run slows to a stutter step-walk and he turns to look for me. I am close enough to reach out and pat his behind.

"It's easier if you hold the rail," I say.

He moves to the side of the steps to take the rail and I hold on too. The wood under my hand is worn smooth from the touch of a million hands, all in an equal search for a way to be safe.

On the third floor, Spencer lets go of the rail and runs to the welcome table, where they serve cookies and coffee. The boy is a homing pigeon when it comes to sweets.

He looks back at me and I hold up my finger for the number one. Spencer takes a cookie and puts it on a napkin.

In one corner, there's a podium where a woman reads aloud from a book. There are about twenty empty chairs and exactly three people who sit in the back. While the woman reads, these people sit and chat among themselves, sipping coffee and eating complimentary cookies.

I rub my whole face with my hand.

You think it will be so wonderful to write and to see your book between hard covers. You believe people will flock to listen to you read from it, but sometimes it's just not that way.

It's like this. People are busy and distracted and most of them just want a place to sit and take a cookie break.

I adjust my bag over my shoulder and check in where the authors are supposed to.

Spencer meets me in the middle of the room and he now has two cookies on his napkin. He lifts them like an offering.

"I got one for you," he says.

"Honey," I say. "You are so sweet."

I take the top cookie, chocolate chip, and take a bite.

"Good?" he says.

"Perfect," I say, my mouth full of cookie that sprays out crumbs.

"Gross," Spencer says. "Eat with your mouth closed."

I laugh and more chunks spray out.

"Eat with your mouth closed," I say and that makes him laugh and spit his own crumbs out at me.

I juggle my bag and cookie in one hand and put a hand on his shoulder.

"Let's find a place to sit," I say.

Spencer brought a collection of Legos in a plastic bag. He pours them out between his legs and they make a rattling sound against the metal seat of his chair.

"Whatcha going to build?" I whisper.

"A rocket car," he says.

"Cool," I say, "did you bring enough stuff?"

Spencer nods and starts in on the assembly.

We are in the back row with the other nonlisteners and our coats hang on the backs of our chairs.

"Our next reader is Jennifer Lauck," a woman says.

She is the medium who introduces each author and she has a worried hostess look in her eyes that she tries to cover with a tight everything-is-going-great smile. Only it isn't going great. The room is too big, the ceiling is too high, and the speakers send out a mash of words scratched with static. Other than the authors, who were scheduled to read months ago, no one is even here. The few who are have faraway looks on their faces.

Spencer has the body of his car together and he adds two wide blue wings.

"Is it a plane too?" I whisper.

He puts one finger to his lips.

"Shhhh," he says. "It's almost your turn."

I roll my eyes and sit back in my chair.

"Jennifer has written two books about her childhood," the lady says and the rest of her words go to static.

Spencer smiles with what looks like pride and it's great having him here. He doesn't care about acoustics or crowds and being next to him makes me not care as much either.

He presses a set of wheels to the back end.

The sound system gets clear again.

"She is a survivor who lived to tell the story of death and abandonment," the lady says. She reads from promotional copy I've heard a thousand times, but am hearing for the first time through Spencer's ears.

"Her mother died when she was seven," the woman says.

Spencer has another set of wheels for the front of his machine, but he stops and looks up at me again.

"Your mother died?" he says.

It's one of those slow-motion, oh my God moments where everything stops.

I open my mouth and close it again and if there was a pause button for life, I'd push it right now. I'd rewind, go back, start over with a better plan, except time doesn't work that way. There is no pause button for life and it's almost always bad timing.

I put my hand on Spencer's head.

"Yeah," I say, "she died."

"When?" he says.

"A long time ago," I say.

The woman is still up there making noise with my name coming up now and then.

I cup the back of Spencer's neck and hold on while he takes this news into the body of a boy whose mother is everything.

His eyes are so wide open, so dark, and so much like my mom in his own way. He has her seriousness, her sense of sweetness and sadness and, like so many people with dark, dark eyes, that look of a person with soul secrets he'll never tell.

Spencer looks down at his flying rocket car, and he looks up at me again.

"I'm so sad for you," he says.

His words bull's-eye my heart where I am still a little kid too.

I clear my throat and it takes everything in me not to cry.

"I'm sad too," I say.

The woman says my name for the last time and I let go of Spencer. I smooth my top, adjust the waistband of my pants, and when I get to the podium, I realize I have no idea what I'm going to read.

There are more people who gather around and I can feel all their eyes looking my way.

I adjust the microphone a little to fit my height, but then I move it away from my face.

"I'm going to read without the microphone," I say.

Spencer is edged over in his chair and his chin lifts to see me up here.

I clear my throat and dig deep for a strong voice.

I read from the beginning, a small passage about a good day with my mother where I brushed her hair and, as I read, I can feel the soft of her between my hands. I can feel the trust we used to share. I can almost smell her body close to me. In the magic of this art, she's alive again.

Spencer is still watching, still listening. It's not how I've been taught about life and death in books or what I've heard in church or even in school, and it's not some New Agey thing that has nine steps attached to healing. It's not even being healed. It's knowing, in my soul, that things are bigger than me. Life and death go beyond what I can know, but they are all here, in a magic language that holds its own truth. My mother is in the words on the page, she's in the sound of my voice, and my love for her lives in my cells. She lives in Spencer too. I see her in his eyes, in his heart, and in the air around him. I can almost see her out there right now, holding him safe on her lap until I'm done.

Spencer puts his flying rocket car into the plastic bag and I pick up the leftover Legos that fell on the floor.

"Is there an elevator here?" he says.

I hold my palm open and his blocks balance in the center of my lifeline.

"You don't want to take the stairs?"

He takes the blocks and puts them into the bag.

"Too many stairs," he says, "I want to push the buttons on the elevator."

I shrug like this is a reasonable request.

"Okay," I say, "let's take the elevator."

I take his bag of Legos and put it into my big purse.

"Do you want another cookie before we go?" I say.

I hold his coat open and he puts his arms in.

"Sure," he says. "Do you want one?"

I zipper him up to his chin and move my hands down to the middle of his body.

"You bet," I say, "something with lots of chocolate."

"I'll get 'em," he says.

I don't let him go though, I keep my hand on the solid feel of him and point to the bank of elevators hidden around the side of the staircase.

"I'll meet you right over there."

He looks in the direction I point.

"Okay," he says.

I open my hands and he runs over to the cookie table.

I put my book into my bag and shrug on my own coat.

When we meet at the elevators, Spencer is already halfway through a chocolate-dipped cookie and there are smears of chocolate around the edges of his mouth.

He holds my cookie in a napkin and when we get into the elevator, he gives it to me.

"Thanks," I say.

"No problem," he says.

Inside the elevator, he pushes the button and the doors

slide to close us in. I reach down and, as if he knows, Spencer reaches up to hold my hand at the same time.

Out of the elevator, he runs through the great entry of the library, past the marble staircase and waits for me at the front door.

After being inside, it's a shock to see all the color of fall again and I squint until I get used to all the yellow and orange and red.

We walk together, eating our cookies and kicking at the leaves.

"You know," I say, "you can ask me anything about my mom and I'll try to tell you, okay?"

Spencer licks the side of his chocolate mouth and squints one eye up at me.

"How did she die?" he said.

I look ahead and think through the complicated story of my mother.

"She couldn't breathe," I say, "she had a hole in her lung, you know where that is, don't you?"

Spencer puts his hand in the middle of his chest and then moves it to the side.

"We're doing the human body at school now."

"Right," I say. "So, her lung was popped by accident and she died because she couldn't breathe."

Spencer kicks and the leaves rise and then fall over the tops of his shoes.

"Where is her body?" he says.

"In Reno," I say, "in a cemetery."

"In a box?" he says.

"No," I say, "she's in a vase."

"Like flowers?" he says.

"Exactly," I say.

We talk about that for a little while, about bodies being put into the ground verses cremated, but how it doesn't hurt because the person, inside, the soul of the person, is gone.

"Where?" he says.

I stop walking and adjust the strap of my bag over my shoulder.

"I don't know, Spencer," I say. "I think about this question a lot though, and I have to believe that the people we love are closer than we think."

"Like ghosts?" he says.

I kneel on one knee and my purse drags on the sidewalk.

"Maybe," I say, "or like something we just can't hold, like water or air."

I move my fingers around at nothing.

"My mom could be right there," I say.

I move my hand between Spencer and me.

"Or right here," I say.

I tilt my head to the side and try to see inside his brain where the wheels turn. My own brain is trying to wrap around the idea too, and I'm fighting against the old way of thinking about death that says the people I love are in some far-off place where I can't see them or touch them. It's a way of thinking that has made me so sad that even today, I can't think of my mother without being next to tears, but now there is a comfort in this way of thinking. Does the comfort mean I'm getting closer to the truth? I don't know, but anything is possible.

Spencer rolls his lips together and there's a tremble there at the corners.

"Are you going to die?" he says.

I move back from him and his question hits me hard. I put my hands on his arms and squeeze down to feel his bones.

"No," I say, shaking my head, "no way."

I talk fast then about how strong I am, how I take good care of my body, and how I'm in perfect health. I say it wasn't that way with my mother, that she was very sick, but then I know I'm lying to him. Healthy or not, my life could end in a heartbeat.

I stop talking and just look into his dark eyes.

When Spencer was born, I made a pact with God by asking if the pain and losses of my life could buy Spencer a life free from pain and loss. It's probably not that different of a pact that all mothers make with some divine force, and in our hearts a part of us wants to believe we struck a real deal. The truth is, God never made any promises to me.

I let go of Spencer's arms and stand up. I brush leaves off my knees and pull my bag over my shoulder. I reach for his hand and he weaves his fingers into mine.

"You know what?" I say.

"What," he says.

"I'm going to do my best not to die, Spencer," I say, "that's all I can do."

Spencer watches the sidewalk, nodding his head, and I wonder what he'll ask next, if he will start to cry or want to know even more, and I don't know if I can answer another question. I still have so many of my own. I'm trying to figure out the story of life and death.

We walk for a long time, just holding hands and kicking leaves and then he squints at something just past my head.

"Look, Mom," he says.

Across the street, there's a house, a yard, and a sidewalk.

"What?" I say.

He noodles his head around like, "Jeez, can't you see."

"What?" I say.

He points.

"That tree is naked," he says.

He makes his voice high and different and puts his arms up in the air to be branches.

"Look at me," he says, "I'm naked. I'm a naked tree."

# PART TWO

# THE PRESENT

*Life is little more than a series of comparisons
between where we are and where we've been.*

—ANON

## BREAST-FEEDING REBEL

Spokane is in Washington State, snuggled against the western edge of Idaho's panhandle. It's not a place that overwhelms the soul. Driving in on I-90 gives little hope there is more to the eye than the dirty ribbon of interstate that passes brick buildings gone black with the soot of time. But in June, look again. In June, the city takes on the scent of true grace that comes with the bloom of the lilac. It could be the hard, cold winters, the rocky soil, or the angle of the sun as it rises and falls on this small stretch of the earth. Whatever happens, when those lilacs bloom, everything in Spokane is sweet and you are glad you are there to smell the air.

Steve and I fell for each other in the spring of the lilac back in '88. Perhaps it was the thick and intoxicating scent of the flower that inspired me to take him home after our third date.

That night, downtown streetlights sent shadows over the businesses with locked doors and closed signs turned out.

Steve touched his hand flat against my stomach and whispered how he wanted me, his breath warm against my ear. I drove through the city, crossing intersections spraypainted in the centers with clusters of lilacs for the Lilac Parade that was coming up in about a week.

I wanted him as much as he wanted me but worried the way a girl worries. Was I thin enough? Would he like the way I looked? Would he mind that I had a couple of flaws?

My apartment was seven blocks from the center of the city, in an old building called the Roosevelt. It had wide green lawns and its own collection of lilac bushes.

I pulled in front of the Roosevelt and as soon as we were out of the car and at the front door of my building, Steve was kissing up the side of my neck.

My car keys were mixed up with my house keys and my hands shook trying to get them sorted out.

I unlocked the door and in the shadows of the entry, Steve pressed me against the row of wall mailboxes and kissed me, that perfect fit of our mouths that felt like a dance. He moved fast though, his hands under my shirt, up my stomach and to my breasts.

He was a layer of fabric away from the parts of my body that worried me the most and I eased his hands down.

"Come on," I said. "Let's go upstairs."

I led him through the lobby, pulled the elevator gate open and pushed four for the top floor.

In the cage of the elevator, Steve was on me again, winding his arms around and pulling me close. I went to him without a question, but as the floors went by, I wanted to send up a flare, offer a warning or maybe a disclaimer that said, "Please disregard these breasts—sure, they have shape, but they don't seem to work quite right."

A friend once told me to never, ever point out a personal physical flaw.

"No one ever notices," she said, "but once you tell them, that's all they see."

I took her advice, kept my mouth shut, and got him into my apartment where the light was low. He was fast to cover the ground he had conquered in the entry and I held my breath while he touched up the skin of my stomach and over my breasts. He wormed under my bra and his fingers searched for nipples.

There was that tiny moment where he stopped moving his hand and touched so careful over the soft of me. I could almost hear the voice in his head that asked, "Where are they?"

They say it happens to people who've had a traumatic birth, something about scar tissue around the areola, but I don't know. Maybe it's a body's own lack of confidence about its place in the world. Maybe I was turned in the way I was as a form of deep shyness that said, "Go away."

In the cooling of that night, June air blew through the sheers of my bedroom window and I couldn't help ask what he thought. I asked in such a subtle way he must have thought I was talking about the size of my breasts rather than the form.

"I like a woman with small breasts," he said, "they're sporty."

I lifted the sheet and looked down at myself. I guess that was true, they didn't have to be different or weird, they could be sporty.

Steve moved his hand over my leg.

"Anyway," he said, "you know what they say?"

"No," I said, "what do they say?"

He smiled this liquid smile of a man relaxed.

"Boobs are for babies," he said, "legs are for men."

I let the sheet go and moved in closer, pressing my sporty chest into his.

"Is that what men are saying these days?"

He lifted his eyebrows up and down on his forehead, flirting, teasing, and in his way, being what I would always admire about Steve, so practical and matter of fact.

"Yep," he said, "that's what they're saying."


"You do plan to breast-feed, don't you?" the nurse said.

"Oh," I said, "I don't know, maybe, maybe not."

So many years later, I was very pregnant with Spencer, having a very different talk about my breasts.

I sat on an examining table with my shirt on, but I was bare from the waist down and covered with a plastic paper for vanity. My stomach was the size of a basketball.

The nurse was named Sara and she was in her cotton uniform of blue pants, blue smock top, and blue footies pulled over her shoes. She was plain but pretty in a clean way, with a wide forehead and her eyes were blue.

She unwrapped the blood pressure thingy and I unbuttoned my shirt at the wrist. I rolled up the sleeve, totally cool even though I hated being on the table with its white sanitary paper that crinkled under my butt. I hated how, very soon, I'd have to endure a pelvic exam.

"Why wouldn't you want to breast-feed?" she said.

I offered up my arm.

"I don't know," I said, "I just haven't thought about it that much."

Sara wrapped the sleeve just above my elbow and did an exaggerated look at my stomach.

"It's probably time to start thinking about it," she said.

I laughed and she laughed, but it was more like this nervous sound between us.

Sara pumped the little bulb and the sleeve tightened on my arm.

Past her was a poster reproduction of a Matisse painting, the line drawing of a hand holding a bouquet of flowers.

Sara put her stethoscope ends into her ears and listened to my blood pulse.

"Good blood pressure," she said.

She let my arm free and wrote numbers in my file.

"About the breast-feeding," Sara said, "you're not sure?"

"Well," I said, "I'm not *not* sure, it's just that, I don't know, I guess I will."

I hated the way my voice came back to me, this hem and haw, and if I were more myself I would have said that I read all about nursing. I knew it was the best thing to do. According to some out there, it was the *only* thing to do. Steve even said I should, since his mother nursed him, but I was having a hard time with the whole idea. I wasn't sure if it was the right thing for me.

Sara leaned against the counter and crossed her arms over herself like we were staying put until we worked the breast-feeding thing out.

"Don't you want to?" she said.

I unrolled my sleeve.

"Sure, I guess I want to, but I'm not sure I can."

I made a big deal of buttoning my shirt at my wrist and talked to the floor.

"I have these strange boobs," I said, "I mean, my boobs aren't strange. I have, uh, you know."

I turned my hands in circles from the wrists, churning for the right words.

Sara didn't seem to understand the language of rotated wrists and tilted her head like a little dog.

I rotated my hands at myself again.

"It's that these," I said, "they go in, not out."

She nodded real slow and then her blue eyes went wide with that ah-ha look.

"Oh," she said, "you've got inverted nipples."

My hand went up like she'd slapped me with the words, but I diverted the flinch into this pseudo eye rub, wondering if everyone in the waiting room got to hear her little announcement.

"Right," I said. "That's right."

She put my file on the counter.

"That's easy to fix," she said.

Opening a drawer, she pulled out two plastic packages.

"These are breast shells," she said.

She unwrapped one of the packages and took out a cone and an O-ring. She snapped the ring into the base of the cone and held it my way.

"Just slip this into your bra," she said, "and wear them until the baby comes."

I took it from her and it was like something you'd see Madonna wear in her underwear-on-the-outside phase.

"Go ahead," Sara said, "give it a try."

The last thing I wanted was to put this thing in my bra, especially in front of her, but I did it anyway, slipping the shell under my shirt and then into my bra.

"There you go," she said, "easy, huh?"

It was easy, but it was hard too. The shell felt cold and terrible and in the reflection of the glass that framed the Matisse poster, I looked like an idiot.

"It doesn't look very natural," I said.

Sara did this wave thing in my direction and put the other shell on the counter.

"Oh," she said, "you hardly notice."

She gathered up my file and left, saying the doctor would be in soon.

When it was just me in the room, I rolled my shoulders back and moved side to side to compare my regular boob to the one with the shell. Sara was nuts. I looked like a fool.

I took the shell out and my boob was back to itself. It was all indented and the nipple hadn't changed much, but I guess you had to wear it longer than three minutes.

I held the breast shell in both my hands and looked past myself to the flowers in the poster.

They were like wildflowers or daisies and I wondered if the bouquet was a gift being offered to someone or if the bouquet would stay with the one who held it.

I turned the shell in my hand, the plastic warm against my skin, and I knew this was part of becoming a mother. This was the unattractive, sacrifice part and it was the right thing to do, but maybe I'd just do it at home, where no one could see me. Maybe that would be enough.

*          *          *

The day after Spencer was born was a Friday and the world felt brand new. Steve had gone home to catch up on lost sleep and Spencer was in the intensive care unit.

I was in a room with mustard yellow walls and was supposed to fill out a bunch of forms, get dressed, and check out of the hospital. I was on drugs that took the edge off the pain, but the side effect was that I'd become a lump without the will to move. There was an ice pack between my legs and I was addicted to both the numbing cold and the bulk of it. Earlier, when a nurse came to refresh the melted ice, I felt what it must be like to be a fighter who had the beating as his prize. I was a mess of raw and swollen flesh.

"Mrs. Lauck?" a voice said.

There was the shadow of a man on the other side of the curtain that had been pulled over the door.

"That's me," I said, my voice smeared and slow.

The shadow pushed aside the curtain and the actual man had wire-rimmed glasses on his face and a manila file under his arm.

"I'm Dr. Gage," he said, "the pediatrician on call."

"Oh," I said, "right."

I patted the side of the bed and found the remote dealy-bobber. I pushed at a button and the bed moved back, I pushed at another button and then the bed raised under my back so I could sit up.

I pushed my hand through my hair, trying to make myself presentable, but I knew my appearance was a mess.

Dr. Gage came to the side of my bed and put his hand out.

I leaned up to put my hand into his but the shake was over

before I could get a good grip. Dr. Gage didn't seem to notice though, he had a fast, restless kind of energy about him, like he was late for something.

His being near me was like a wake-up shot of espresso and my mind cleared.

He pulled the file from under his arm and opened it like a book.

"I just saw your, ah . . ." he looked down at the chart.

"Son," I said.

"Right," he said, "son, ah . . ."

"Spencer," I said.

"Right," he said, "six weeks early, right?"

"Yes," I said, "my son Spencer is six weeks early."

His eyes moved around on the pages in the file, searching for something. I moved on the bed, adjusting pillows behind my back to be as upright as I could be.

"It's hard to believe he's premature," Dr. Gage said. "He looks just great. Strong heart. Good lungs. I've looked him over top to bottom and everything checked out."

If I knew Dr. Gage better, I would have pulled him down and given him a big bear hug.

"That's wonderful," I said, "because I just got checked out and I didn't know if I'd have to go home and leave him here."

Dr. Gage scratched at the side of his face.

"Oh, you will have to leave him here," he said, "at least for a few days."

I put my hand over the bones of my chest.

"Why?" I said.

"We have to run a few more tests," he said, "and we should watch him for jaundice."

He didn't talk directly to me, he talked to the pages in the file, like it was a script prepared for him.

"And, at thirty-four weeks, he probably won't have the suck and swallow reflex," he said, "so the nurse will be tube feeding him later today."

I jerked up so fast, something tore down below.

"You want to do *what?*"

Dr. Gage shifted his weight from one foot to the other.

"It's standard," he said, "we do it all the time." He detailed how they would put the tube down my baby's throat, but I shook my head while he talked and moved my hair behind my ears.

"No, no, no," I said, "I don't think so. No sir, you are not putting a tube down his throat."

Dr. Gage's glasses slipped down his nose and he pushed them back up with his index finger.

"I haven't even tried to nurse him, we have no idea if he can suck and swallow or not," I said, "and besides, wouldn't it be better to try a bottle first, at least to see?"

I talked fast and moved my hands around to make my point.

"Not that I want to give him a bottle, since I was going to try to nurse, but I read that the baby just needed a little of that premilk stuff, you know, what is it called?"

"Colostrum," Dr. Gage said.

I flipped my hand in the air between us.

"Right," I said, "technically he just takes a little of that stuff, technically he doesn't need to eat for, what? It's like three to five days?"

"Right," Dr. Gage said, "but you might not produce milk for six more weeks."

His words made me stop with the gestures.

"Six weeks?" I said. "Are you sure about that?"

"Well," he said, "it's when you were due, but you could get it to come in sooner, maybe."

It was quiet then and a shake came into my arms and legs and there was this tired feeling in my bones. If it were just me, I'd lie down and sleep for a week, but Spencer was waiting for me. That was another part of being a mother. I had to do whatever I could to help him.

Dr. Gage closed Spencer's file and held it to his chest.

"Well, tell me how," I said, "tell me how to get my milk to come in."

Two hours later, I was checked out of my room, doped up on quadruple-strength Tylenol, and hooked up to a mega bovine sucking machine. It was a mean steel box attached to a podium on wheels with knobs that controlled the flow of pressure from low to high. Plastic tubes were attached to the pump and they ran to these funnel cups I held over my breasts.

The machine inhaled and exhaled, mostly the nipples, forcing them out in a way that even the nipple shells didn't.

I was in this side room just off the intensive care unit, a space set aside for the parents of premature babies. The walls were a mint green and there was enough furniture for a few people to sit. On the side table, there was a vase of silk flowers and over the sofa, there were two watercolor poster prints of the Pacific Ocean.

I was set up here by a nurse named Lynn, a beefy girl who hailed from the Midwest, a bit of trivia Lynn announced while manhandling my virgin breasts into the funnel cups of the machine.

"Don't you worry, Jennifer," she said, "my father had a farm. I know all about getting a momma to make milk."

I guess Lynn figured, with my boobs in her hands and all, she ought to tell this kind of stuff about herself, which included how she wasn't married, never intended on getting married, and never, ever planned to have children.

"Nothing will break you of wanting a baby faster than working here," she said.

Where was Lynn back when Steve and I decided to conceive?

I didn't even let myself think that way or if I did think things like that, they were shoved down with other nasty thoughts, like how much easier it would be to scoop a couple jiggers of formula into a bottle, add water, and shake or that the tube feeding Dr. Gage was talking about actually seemed humane in retrospect.

My boobs, so soft and round and lovely before (even with their mutant nipples), were being inhaled and exhaled into long tube extensions of my chest. Looking at myself under the power of the pump made me want to laugh out loud and burst into tears.

The only good news was how drops of gold fluid were coming from my shy nipples, which Lynn celebrated as evidence that my body was ready to make milk. To get it to come faster, Lynn had me on a schedule to pump for twenty minutes, every three hours.

Between my appointments, Lynn suggested I go to the store and get a couple of good-size bras.

"You'll need at least a G cup," she said.

"A G cup?" I said. "That's like five cup sizes bigger than I am now. Do they even make such a thing?"

Lynn pushed her ample chest out with farm girl pride.

"You bet they do," she said.

And they did.

In twenty-four hours my breasts were honeydew melons that barely fit my new G-cup bra.

And milk?

Under Lynn's careful care, I had enough to feed every baby in the hospital.

Then I had to learn how to nurse.

I sat on the sofa in the side room and cradled Spencer in my arm. One huge boob popped out of the peekaboo door of the maternity bra, but even after all that pumping, my nipple presented less than impressive.

Even Lynn looked a little disappointed, which she turned into this deep sigh, shrug, smile combination.

To be all hung out like this was embarrassing, but I shoved that down. I had read all the books by all the experts that said I should breast-feed, and I was going to breast-feed because that is what a good mother did.

"Now squeeze his cheeks together with one hand," Lynn said, "make his mouth pucker up, and then move him in."

I did exactly like she said, but it was a lot like driving a stick shift car for the first time, there was so much to think about with the clutch and the gears and the gas. It was awkward to hold Spencer, with all his tubes coming from his arm and head and not pull anything out. It was even harder to swivel his head in the direction of dinner and simultaneously coerce him to open his mouth.

"Bring him in closer," Lynn said, "lower him a little, that's good, now pull him on."

I hung in there with the directions, but after I turned Spencer's head to my breast for the sixth time, he pulled his face into one big wrinkle and cried.

"I don't think he's interested," I said.

Lynn had her hands at her round hips, truly perplexed.

She had short brown hair cut like a man's and eyes I couldn't figure out. Sometimes they were dark green, sometimes they were blue, but it wasn't just the color of her eyes, it was the way she came through them. She was this person who was also two colors, one a professional who wanted to get things done, but also a person who seemed to really care.

"Let him calm down," Lynn said, "and we'll try again."

I held Spencer against my shoulder and rubbed circles on his back until he stopped crying, and then went through the whole juggling act again, but this time Spencer didn't even try. He fixed a look on me with his tiny dark eyes that said, "Don't you get it, woman? Leave me alone." Then he let out this combination of cry and scream that made my arms shake and lifted a film of sweat under my clothes.

I moved Spencer to my shoulder and rubbed his back again.

"I'm sorry," I said, "I don't think I can do this."

While my son cried, I couldn't help it, the tears were out of me too.

Lynn kneeled to where I sat on the sofa and put her hand on my knee.

"If we give him a bottle," Lynn said, "at least we'll know if he can suck and swallow and really, that's what Dr. Gage needs."

On the side table was a bottle of my milk I had to pump off to get my breasts to deflate. I should just give it to him, but then what kind of mother couldn't nurse her own baby. I'd be a complete failure even before I started. I shook my head and nodded at the same time, unable to make a decision for myself and it was Lynn who did it for me. She got the bottle of breast milk and pulled a few tissues from a box, handing both my way.

"Don't worry," Lynn said, "we'll get him on the breast later."

A day later, the little side room off the intensive care unit was like a home for Steve and me. We had both been to our real home, for sleep and supplies, but we couldn't leave Spencer at the hospital by himself. It didn't matter that all the best doctors and nurses were there to take care of him, we needed to stay close so we just camped out.

Steve was slouched in the sofa cushions and his feet were up on the coffee table. He had Spencer on his chest, patting at his back with one hand while, in the other, he had the remote control for the TV. Steve snapped through, weather, stock market, news, and then stopped on some cooking show.

I was on the sofa too, my feet up on the table, but I was held in place by compresses, both hot and cold.

My breasts were still growing and were so hard, it hurt to think about them. Lynn confessed that we might not have needed to pump so much and she felt so bad, she wrapped my boobs in hot towels to take the edge off.

My legs were swollen too, which was the side effect of walking too soon after having a baby. I'd been to the mall to buy bras, I'd been home to get a couple hours of sleep, and I'd been walking the long hospital halls back to be with Spencer, to pump my boobs, and to try to nurse.

It had only been two days since Spencer was born, but these two days felt like two years and all my good mothering had landed me on my ass, swollen, in pain, and so tired I could barely keep my eyes open.

Steve turned the channels and looking over at him made me angry the way you can get when you're suffering alone. He was all relaxed with the baby on his chest and I was a wreck.

"I should just give up on breast-feeding," I said.

Steve moved his head on the sofa to look my way.

"Isn't it a little late to decide now?" he said. "Isn't your milk in?"

I narrowed up my eyes.

On the TV, a weatherwoman pointed to a map and said a cold front was coming in.

"What?" Steve said.

"Nothing," I said.

"Don't be mad," he said.

"I'm not mad," I said.

"I know when you're mad, Jen," he said.

I just kept my focus on the TV and Steve flipped the channel to a home renovation show.

There was a knock at the door and Lynn's voice was over my head.

"How's it going in here?" she asked.

I tilted my head back and Lynn was upside down.

"Could it get any worse?" I said.

Lynn laughed at my miserable mood and that was what I had liked about her all along. She didn't judge me, she just tried to help.

She came the rest of the way in then, the grind of working

a double shift in her eyes that were more blue now than green.

"I've got something for you," she said.

She came down on my side of the sofa and her big girl self curled into a surprisingly good squat. She balanced her elbow on her knee and opened her hand to show two small square packages.

"These are called nipple shields," she said.

She looked around like someone might be listening and made her voice low.

"The lactation people hate when we give these out, but I think you need a break."

She put one of the packages on the side table next to the sofa and peeled the other package open, taking out a thin plastic thing that looked like a nipple prophylactic except it had three holes in the tip.

"It's shaped like the nipple on a bottle," she said, "which we know Mr. Fussy over there loves."

She nodded at the sleeping Spencer.

"Put this over your breast and voilà," she said. "I bet anything he latches right on."

I looked from her to the shield and to her face again. Her eyes were full of a knowing I didn't have. I took the nipple shield between my fingers and the plastic was so thin, it weighed almost nothing.

Steve looked at it too and smiled.

"There you go, Jen," he said.

I wanted to tell him to mind his own damn business, but I didn't. I just turned the nipple shield this way and that, looking through the three little holes in the tip.

"Why do lactation people hate it?" I said.

Lynn balanced her hands on her knees and shook her head.

"I have no idea," she said. "They are a great invention and they really help, but they're pretty new and some people say they aren't natural, they say they promote nipple confusion; you know, you've read all that information too."

I lowered the nipple shield to rest on the wad of towels spread over my chest.

"You really think it will work?" I said.

"It can't hurt," she said.

Lynn patted my knee and smiled and there was something in her laying of hands on me, it was a silent message between women.

Lynn had been around enough mothers and babies to know what would be coming for me. She knew I would meet a lactation specialist who would insist the shield was wrong and would put me through another run of latch-on hell, convinced that I just needed to learn how to do it right. She knew I would go home, try to nurse without the nipple shield, and that Spencer would latch on, but wouldn't latch right since I didn't have great nipples. She knew there would be pain and cracking and bleeding and that I would covertly use the nipple shield, all the while feeling like a terrible mother. She knew that the entire time I nursed Spencer, which would be six months of hell, I would cry a river of frustrated tears, since I was one of those women who tried too hard, who always wanted to do the right thing, and who took the advice of experts as if they somehow channeled their instructions direct from God. She also knew that when I had another baby, I would remember what worked and what didn't work. I would be smarter and stronger and I wouldn't care what other people said. Thanks to Lynn, I'd remember about the nipple shield and I'd nurse for six months of heaven with Josephine that would wipe clean the hell of getting it so wrong with Spencer.

I couldn't guess the future, of course, and maybe Lynn couldn't either, but something passed between us and it was that kind of magic.

Lynn put the package for the nipple shield on the side table and stood up.

"There's an extra one," she said, "but you can buy them at some baby stores."

I wished I wasn't under hot towels and cold ice. I wished I could stand and hug her, but instead, I put my hand out.

"Thank you, Lynn," I said, "I really appreciate all your help."

She smiled all the way into those blue-green eyes and took my hand. For a farmgirl, she had such soft hands.

"It's my job," she said. "Good luck."

# GETTING THE BLUES

Josephine lies in her bassinet, hands in fists at each side of her head. Her skin is that soft pink from inside a shell, her hair is flax shining gold, and behind those bone china eyelids threaded with delicate veins, her eyes are forget-me-not blue. She's a sleeping beauty.

I stand over her. I stand near her. I stand one cry away and wait for that moment she'll need me again.

Steve and Spencer have gone to the park and the day stands at the time between afternoon and evening. Outside, dusk shadows lift, but move so slow you barely notice if you aren't as still as I am, the way a mother gets when she's waiting to be needed.

As the day changes, there is a pace change inside me too. It's a tempo drop from the back of my neck and down my spine to stop at my heart, and when it gets there, to my heart, there will be a sound to go with the change. The sound will be as sad and as slow as a sorrowful woman singing the blues.

I look at my watch, a habit of mine to digitally confirm that sure enough, it's 4:30. Four-thirty marks the beginning of the witching hours that burn inside of me.

I lift a pink blanket to cover Josephine and her milk-sweet smell is all around me.

"Safe journey, baby," I whisper.

I go into the kitchen then, turn on the fire under the teapot, and watch the blue flicker of the flame.

Five years ago, Spencer slept in that same bassinet, but back then I didn't listen to the blues. Back then, I was all techno, retro, go, go, go. I worshiped the tick-tock of the clock and had each day mapped on a pad of legal paper with the words "To Do" written at the top.

I started all this when I worked in television news with its schedules and deadlines. I was a reporter and then a producer, in charge of everyone and everything. After six years of that world, I perfected the craft of being busy and took my efficiency with me to start a business out of my house.

While I was pregnant with Spencer, I kept the efficiency, but let my business go so I could study at the local college, first mediation and then writing. I wasn't sure what I wanted to do and thought, a baby would be a nice break from the whole career track, a baby would help me shift my focus and see what it was I really wanted.

Steve was all for it. Deep down, he was an old-fashioned boy who believed a woman's place was home with her kids, like his mom and his mother's mother before her. Deep down, I was an old-fashioned girl too. I believed it was the best thing for a woman to stay with her baby, at least at the beginning during the whole bonding and breast-feeding thing.

There I was homebound with Spencer and come 7:00 A.M., I got up, made the bed, took a shower, and got dressed even though I had nowhere to go. I may have had three hours of sleep the night before, but it didn't matter to me, the routine was everything, or at least everything I understood.

One morning, I was up doing my thing and Spencer was sleeping. We were six weeks into each other, him as a baby, me as a mom, and the lack of sleep was messing with my sense of reality.

I had never met this kind of tired before and had no idea that a side effect of no sleep would be a yellow jacket nest of resentment and anger. I also had no idea that under this nest lived deeper feelings of sadness and even loneliness that would make a therapist salivate.

To my mind, it all made no sense. I wasn't sad. I wasn't lonely. I was the busy one, I was the girl with a plan and a To Do list.

That morning, that tired, everything changed.

I stood near Spencer's bassinet, on call the way I was learning to be. His baby mouth was open just a little and his dark lashes were curled in the hollows of his eyes. It was his dead man's sleep. I lifted his arm and it dropped like a rock. He'd be out for at least an hour, maybe longer.

I tucked a blanket around his small body and left him to sleep.

In the bathroom, I left the door open enough to hear if he cried and turned on the shower. While the water warmed, I got undressed to reveal a body that wasn't mine anymore. It was this mother's skin that still didn't fit my image of myself. My heavy breasts sloshed with milk and my stomach and hips were so soft they shifted with every step.

I got into the shower and shut the door.

A while back, Steve had a plumber put the showerhead up an extra twelve inches. He said he needed it high to make up for all the years he showered in stalls where the water hit him in the center of his chest. He liked how the spray hit him now, but whenever I got in after Steve took a shower, the water came over me like mist.

I wrestled with the knob on the showerhead and the water funneled from a mist into an equally unsatisfying stream. I stood there thinking evil thoughts about Steve and his stupid shower.

I took the soap and turned it over in my hands. I hated him for having a shower he liked. I hated he was working away at his job. I hated how his life hadn't changed at all and my life was completely different

Next, I hated myself. Wasn't I the one who agreed to stay home? Wasn't I the old-fashioned girl?

Then I was just feeling sorry for myself and mad melted into tears.

I put my face into the water.

With my hands all lathered up, I put the soap in the dish and washed over my shoulders, down my arms, and into my armpit.

Under there, I stopped.

Under there, it was a lump, a hell of a lump.

I touched around the thing over and over and it was the size of jawbreaker.

What the hell was it?

In my other armpit, there was another lump.

Jesus, you have cancer.

I shut the water off and got out of the shower. Water and soap ran down my legs. I pulled a towel off the rack and walked foot pools from the bathroom to the bedroom. Spencer still slept in infant oblivion and I flipped on a monitor to hear him downstairs.

I moved so quiet, trying not to disturb his rest while voices in my head whispered, Cancer, cancer, cancer.

I closed the door with a soft click and when it was just me, I ran.

In the living room there was a pile of books, *Your Baby, The New Mommy,* and then the bible on boobs: *Breast-feeding Basics.* I pulled it from the pile and stood there, dripping water. I looked in the index for "lumps," and found a passage that read: *Lumps could indicate a serious condition. Call your doctor right away.*

Our living room had a big picture window and the drapes were pulled wide. Outside, the world drove by and the overly friendly mailman was headed up our drive.

I fisted the towel tighter between my breasts and took the book into my office.

The room had been transformed since Spencer was born. We had a spare bed where Steve was sleeping on the nights he had to work and where I tried to get a quick nap. My desk had been shoved into a corner and was piled over with junk mail. The computer and printer were covered with plastic protectors and it had been so long since I had removed them, the protectors were thick with a layer of dust.

Through the receiver of the baby monitor, I could hear Spencer breathe even and slow and I threw *Breast-feeding Basics* on the bed. I moved the piles of junk mail and, under one big pile, found my Rolodex. I opened its plastic door and flipped the dial to W.

I dialed the number and with the phone balanced between my bare shoulder and ear, shoved wet hair back from my head. Water dripped down my neck and between my shoulder blades.

"Women's Health," a woman said.

My whole body shook, but I tried to keep my voice calm and professional as I talked about the lumps under my arms, asking if I could speak to the nurse.

I was put on hold for what seemed like an eternity, and then a familiar voice came on the line.

"Hello, Jennifer, this is Kathleen," said the nurse. "You found a lump?"

Kathleen wasn't a friend, but back when I was pregnant she had seen me at the clinic, measured my stomach, and laughed when I cracked my stupid jokes. She was familiar enough that when I heard her friendly voice, I let myself drop the professional act.

"Oh, Kathleen, thank goodness," I said.

I touched up into my arm again, like showing her through the phone.

"Under my arm," I said. "Under both arms."

All of my body shook down to my feet and the tears were coming on strong.

"I can't find anything in the book about this except it might be serious."

"Jennifer," Kathleen said, "slow down."

"What if it's cancer?" I said.

"Hold on, Jennifer," Kathleen said.

"I can't have cancer," I said, sobbing between my words, "I just can't."

"Jennifer," Kathleen said, her voice firm and strong, "you do not have cancer."

My knees were giving out under me and I pulled the chair from behind my desk, sitting down on a pile of old newspapers.

"Okay?" Kathleen said. "You don't have cancer, you are fine."

I sniffed hard and wiped my face with the corner of my towel.

"Okay," I said, my voice small.

She talked in a calm way and explained that the lumps under my arms were probably milk backed up in my lymph glands. She said it was completely normal. She said I should pump a little milk and try hot compresses.

Riding her voice, I was back down on earth, breathing deep and even again.

"Thank you, Kathleen," I said.

I wiped my whole face with my hand and my head felt light.

"Wow, I got really scared."

"Yes," she said, "you did."

Kathleen cleared her throat.

"Where is your baby right now?" she said.

"The baby?" I said.

"Is he there with you?"

"Yes," I said, "he's asleep, upstairs. I have the monitor with me."

"Okay," she said, "and is anyone helping you?"

"No, no one is here, it's just me," I said.

Kathleen's questions were more professional than friendly and I moved the telephone from one ear to the other.

"What are you getting at, Kathleen?" I said.

She was quiet a moment and then she cleared her throat.

"I just want to make sure your baby is safe," she said.

"Why wouldn't he be safe?" I said.

I could hear that bland music of a doctor's office playing in the background.

"I'm not saying he isn't safe," she said, "but you are clearly fragile, I can hear it in your voice."

"I'm not fragile," I said, "I was frightened about these lumps, you should feel them, they are huge."

I fingered the lumps again and it was true, they were very big lumps.

"You might have postpartum depression," she said.

"What?" I said, letting the lumps go.

"It's normal," Kathleen said, "sometimes we call it the blues."

Kathleen listed the symptoms:

If I experienced any previous traumas in my life, I could have the blues.

If the birth of my son had been traumatic, I could have the blues.

If I felt overwhelmed by the change in my life, I could have the blues.

I interrupted her.

"Look," I said, "I'm not depressed. I've never been depressed in my life. I'm the happiest person I know."

"You don't want to ignore this," Kathleen said, "it happens to a lot of women."

"I'm not ignoring anything," I said. "I'm not depressed."

"You might think about joining a Mommy's Group," she said.

"I'm not depressed," I said.

"I'm going to give you a number to call," she said.

"Look, I told you, I'm not depressed," I said.

I held the telephone so tight, it hurt my hand.

"Do you have a pen?" Kathleen asked.

I let out a deep sigh, giving in and pulled a pen out from the mess of paper on my desk.

"I'll take the number," I said, "but like I said, I am not depressed."

July was wet that year and the rain fell every hour with twenty-minute breaks in between. That night Steve came home, we ate dinner, and when the clouds parted, took a walk.

Steve had our dog at the end of a leash. I had Spencer in his sling, which was a length of fabric that went around my neck and swaddled him tight.

The air was warm and sweet with summer rain and when we got around the corner from our house, the dog stopped to sniff where fresh-mowed grass met sidewalk. Steve and I stopped too.

Steve wore an all-weather raincoat and a pair of shorts, even though it was still cold. Shorts were a principle to Steve. You started wearing them in June and didn't stop wearing them until the frosts of November.

"I had a breakdown today," I said.

"What do you mean, breakdown?" Steve said.

I put a hand on his arm, the cool slick of his rain jacket against my skin.

"Not a breakdown," I said, "more like a meltdown. Not a meltdown really, a crisis, no not a crisis, more like a situation."

Steve's blue eyes squinted to see past my words and he had small wrinkles that fanned out, making him look older than he was.

"Not even a situation," I said, "it was more like an incident."

"What happened?" Steve said. His voice was restless for me to get to the point.

It helped to sway side to side with my arms around Spencer and while I did this, I told the whole story about the lumps and the nurse.

"I disagree with her," I said, "I'm not depressed, it's just that I don't feel like myself, I'm weepy and sad and very tired."

Steve moved his hand over his face, rubbing down around his chin.

"Do you think you'd hurt the baby?" he said.

I looked at him for such a long time, looking for compassion or even empathy, but Steve didn't have those feelings in his eyes.

"Forget it, Steve," I said.

I walked up the sidewalk and left him there.

"Hey," he said, "wait."

I didn't stop though. I was crying and trying not to cry at the same time.

I pushed at the tears, shoving them away, and Steve picked up the dog like she was a football and caught up with me.

"Wait," he said.

"I don't want to talk to you," I said.

He reached out then and took ahold of my arm, which I shook off. I didn't want him to touch me either.

"Jen," he said, "come on."

Whenever Steve feels soft toward me, he always calls me Jen.

Even though I was still mad, I stopped and pushed my tears away.

We stood on the sidewalk, together but apart, and I looked at my feet on the sidewalk.

"It's normal to be worried, isn't it?" he said.

I pinned a look at him, one of those deep looks that goes into a person's soul, and I wiped at my face again.

"How long have you known me, Steve?" I said.

Steve licked his lips, nervous under my stare down and he searched the sky.

"I don't know," he said, "seven years now."

Carmel was between us, her dark brown eyes watching me with the pure adoration only a dog can muster. I petted over her soft blonde head.

"In seven years, have I ever hurt anyone or anything?" I said. "Have I ever hurt the dog or you?"

Steve rolled his eyes in that way he did when I was right. He put the dog down on her feet and she scurried off to sniff at a tree.

"You tell me you freaked out," he said. "I worry, that's all."

Around us was our neighborhood with its tree-lined streets, old houses, and lawns trimmed with perfect edges. I threw my arms up, the way you do when you are fed up.

"I didn't 'freak out' all over the baby, Steve," I said. "He was sleeping upstairs. Jeez, give me a little credit here."

Steve rolled his lips together and didn't say anything else. Who knew what he was thinking. With my tears and anger and now, gesturing like some kind of wild woman, he probably thought I was a nut.

The dog ran ahead, pulling her leash all the way out, and we walked a little ways, together, but not together. Steve put a hand around my shoulder, squeezing in a little, like he was trying to pep talk me.

"I'm sorry, Jen," he said, "if you're not worried, I'm not worried. Okay?"

I nodded like, "Okay, fine," but deep down, I was worried. Maybe something *was* wrong with me. Maybe being sad meant you were depressed and depression meant you could change the core of your character to be a person who would hurt a child.

A mist fell around us and overhead the sky got dark again. Steve pulled his hood up over his head and I did the same.

I moved my hands up and down over Spencer's back. He was so tiny and fragile. I knew I'd never hurt him, not for anything in the world, but maybe I would. Maybe I didn't know myself at all.

The mist turned to a full-on rain and Steve ran ahead with the dog. I pulled the folds of the sling together, keeping Spencer from getting wet, but I didn't run to get out of the rain. I walked slow and careful steps and by the time I got to the house, I decided I'd try, for Spencer's sake, to talk to other women. It wasn't for Kathleen or Steve. I'd do it for the baby.

*     *     *

The hospital was just six blocks from our house, but it took a Herculean effort to get out the door and walk that far. There was all of Spencer's stuff to pack, blankets, toys, extra diapers, and wipes and then Spencer cried the whole way. I had to carry him in one arm and push the stroller with the other hand. By the time I got to my first mommy group meeting, I was soaked with sweat and my head felt like a drum that Spencer's cries had beat apart.

I parked the stroller outside the closed door of a conference room where a sign read NEW MOMMY GROUP.

With Spencer in one arm, I used the other to take up the baby bag, a blanket, the pacifier, and a developmentally approved rattle.

I opened the door to fluorescent light so white that shadows didn't stand a chance. There was a group of women who formed a circle on the floor and in front of each was a single baby afloat on his or her own blanket island.

There was one table and a woman without a baby who leaned against it. Her nametag said CAROLYN and she had dark hair that curled around her face. Behind her, flyers were printed on sheets of pastel-colored paper and stacked in neat piles.

"Hi there," she said, "you must be a new mommy."

I readjusted my stuff over my shoulder and freed up a hand to give Carolyn a thumbs-up.

"Well, come on in," Carolyn said.

I let the door close behind me, found an open spot at the opposite end of the room, and shook out a blanket for Spencer.

I sat on the floor cross-legged and it wasn't hard to fit in. I was chubby, I had a baby, I was a woman. Across from me, a mother shook her rattle at her baby's hand. I picked up Spencer's rattle and did the same. So far, so good.

"Okay, ladies and babies," Carolyn said, "welcome."

She started a round-robin discussion, asking each woman to introduce herself, her baby, and to ask a question.

"Anything you want," Carolyn said, "I'm here to help."

The first woman in the circle was small with dark straight hair.

"Hi," she said, putting her hand on her chest, "I'm Jill, this is Sage."

"Hi, Jill," Carolyn said. "Hi, Sage."

"Hi, Jill," we all said. "Hi, Sage."

Jill smiled and said hi again and then reported how Sage was doing just great. She was sleeping through the night, she was so happy, but she had some excessive drool.

Carolyn listened in this intent way, her fist under her chin that was pushed forward to Jill. Her full attention even made little dents of concern at the corners of her eyes.

"Oh dear," Carolyn said, "is it just drool, or is her nose running too?"

"No, just drool," Jill said.

Carolyn searched the table.

"Okay, that's just teething," Carolyn said.

She pulled a yellow flyer and passed it down to Jill.

"You should see a little tooth in no time," Carolyn said.

"Great," Jill said, taking the page, satisfied.

"Hi everyone," the next woman said, "I'm Becky and this is Jack."

"Hi, Becky," Carolyn said. "Hi, Jack."

"Hi, Becky," everyone said. "Hi, Jack."

Becky talked about how Jack was rolling over and a couple of the women clapped as if this were cause for true celebration.

"He has a little rash though," Becky said. "It just started."

Carolyn put that fist to her chin again and nodded.

"Oh dear," Carolyn said, "is it like a hive with small red marks on the skin or an overall red rash?"

"More like a hive," Becky said.

Carolyn moved the papers around on the table and pulled a blue sheet.

"It could be a food allergy," Carolyn said, passing the sheet down to Becky. "Are you doing solids yet?"

There was a long discussion about Becky's diet and possible allergens in her breast milk and somewhere in the middle, I zoned out. All of these women were in various stages of bouncing, rocking, swaddling, and breast-feeding and I wondered, Who are these people? Did any of them feel overwhelmed? Did they miss their lives from before? Did they think about anything beyond diaper rash and drool?

The conversation with Becky ended and was over to another woman, who reported that her Justin was also sleeping through the night and how much of a delight he was, how she felt so blessed and full of love and really, she had no problems or questions.

"I just wanted to share that," she said.

Around me, women nodded and smiled, the room practically purred, and Carolyn took the moment of golden glow to talk about how fast the baby stage goes, how it's hard for a new mother to really savor every moment, but that we should try.

"Once they get bigger," she said, "you'll never get this back."

Spencer made his fussy sounds and I dropped the rattle and pulled him into my arms. His body snuggled into mine, his face wormed into the soft part of my neck, and the feel of him was so nice. Justin's mother was right. What planet was I on? Why wasn't I just savoring and appreciating and feeling blessed? What was wrong with me?

By the time the group came around to where we were, there had been long talks about where to get clothes at an affordable price, the various techniques for burping a baby, and the high cost of formula. There was no discussion of the blues. Not one.

Next to me, a mother nursed her baby and talked about how her little Emma adored mangoes and pears, but she wondered if organic was better than the more commercial brands. My own hello was moments away and I could just see it.

"Hi, I'm Jennifer," I'd say, "this is Spencer."

"Hi, Jennifer," Carolyn would say. "Hi, Spencer."

"Hi, Jennifer," everyone would say. "Hi, Spencer."

"Yeah," I'd say, "well, Spencer is six weeks old now and he sleeps a lot, but I'm not sleeping at all, which is okay. Like Becky over there, I'm really lucky to have him considering the hell of his birth, the eight days in the hospital, the whole premature thing, but I'm not complaining, no, it's just that I'm feeling a little odd right now, that's why I'm here. I miss my old body, my old life, sleep, and freedom. I feel sad all the time, waves of sadness that seem to have no end, and when I talk about them, when I try to figure it all out, my husband is sure that I'm going to hurt the baby or something so, I guess that's my question, I'm just wondering, can you help me here? Do you think I'm losing my mind?"

I could see the moment after I shut up. I could see the energy in this lifeless room shift, could see the eyes of all the women flatten and the mouths fall open. Even the babies would stop making noise. Carolyn too. Carolyn would do a complete blank, not for long, but long enough for me to know there was nothing on the table about insanity today.

Oh dear.

I didn't talk about it, of course not, I asked some stupid question about disposable diapers verses cloth and had to carry a fussy Spencer all the way home.

It was almost eight months later that I was driving over the Columbia River and heard something new about the blues.

Spencer was in the back, sleeping in his car seat and I was on the way to a mall, doing research for a freelance article I was writing for a local newspaper.

I was listening to a doctor from Australia talk on the radio. She was discussing postpartum depression. "What's this about calling it 'the blues,' " she said. "Try black and blue, think heroin withdrawal, think hormonal hell, and *that's* the blues."

God, she was funny, she spoke in a way that had no apology and complete authority. She said postpartum was worse for American women because of the stigma of mental illness and I wanted to stand up in her audience, wherever she was, and say, "Sister, you are so right."

The blues held me hostage for five months, mostly because I told myself they weren't there at all. Sleep deprivation made them worse, but then when Spencer started to sleep through the night, the blues went away.

It seemed so simple, but it was true, and once they were gone I was left with a lot to think about. All the feelings of being trapped and of sadness and loneliness, were feelings amped up on hormones, but they were still true feelings connected to real problems I needed to fix.

The blues made me change from the old-fashioned mother who was home all the time to the kind of mother I needed to be. I got Steve to help more, I went back to work, I got plenty of sleep, and I took time for myself. It wasn't easy, I was still trying to find my way, but it was a start.

"What women need to do," the radio doctor said, "is be kind to themselves. When they've just had a baby, they should put their feet up and let people bring them tea and cookies. They should just try to relax."

By the time she finished talking, I was well across the Columbia River, but I was different. She was right, and I knew if I ever had another baby and went through those terrible blues, I'd do things different.

Here I am with another baby and I am doing things different. First, I don't try to tell myself that this isn't happening.

I'm not sure if I am depressed, but I do feel strange and sad.

While Josephine sleeps, I palm my teacup and look out the window at the world of our new neighborhood, a place we moved to about six months ago.

It's nice here. It's quiet and safe and since having Josephine, I've met a whole new circle of mothers who are like all the other mothers I've met before. Not one of them admits to feeling sad or even slightly depressed.

I know, I've asked and the answer is always the same. "No, not me."

Between my having Spencer and then Josephine, a woman drowned all five of her children, one by one in a bathtub, and her defense was postpartum depression. Her crime got people talking about postpartum and now you can go online and find thousands of websites filled with information, but it also seemed to confirm the collective fear and deepen the stigma. We are still at the place where depression is one step from insanity. We're still at the place where women are afraid to talk, and to me, that seems like the crazy part.

So every afternoon, I don't talk to the women on my street. I don't call anyone on the telephone. I don't drag myself to any Mommy Groups. Every afternoon, I'm inside with a cup of tea trying to be kind to myself, trying not to judge, trying not to be afraid. I sit with my feelings instead, and here is what they look like to me.

Having the blues is like standing in a powerful surf. The waves are feelings of having no control, of sadness, of loneliness, and of being horribly misunderstood. These emotions push gravity against my body, which tries to hold on to its place here on earth. I might try to adjust, try to set my feet wide, but it doesn't matter because the power of the feelings always seems to win, it just takes me where it wants me to go.

It's a whole hour later, 5:30 by my watch, and my tea is gone. I sit in a big easy chair by the window, the day falling to night and yes, I'm all blue and strange and out of whack.

Steve and Spencer come up the walk, Spencer running

ahead with his jacket flung behind him like a superhero cape.

He sees me up here and waves his arms over his head.

Steve looks up and waves too.

Steve still doesn't understand this mysterious world I'm in. Maybe it's the emotion that makes him so uncomfortable, maybe it's the differnce between being a man and woman, I don't know. This time, he's different too. He cooks for us, he cleans up after, and he even asks if I need a refill on my tea. He's trying to help and in trying, he does help.

The baby makes her sound and I put my teacup on the coffee table.

Steve is going to make dinner tonight. I will hold the baby and read Spencer a book and then I'll put the baby down and make sure I get enough sleep. These blues will go away at about 7:30 and I will be myself again, the same but different. I will have gone through them almost completely alone and I will have many new lessons to learn about myself.

I walk through the kitchen to the dining room and in her bassinet, Josephine pushes up and looks around like, "What is this place?"

I lift her, taking up the pink blanket to keep her warm, and I fold her into my arms.

"Hi, baby," I say, touching the tip of my finger to the end of her nose, "welcome back to earth."

# WHAT HAUNTS THE NIGHT

There is pressure between my eyes, this push of a finger that won't give up and Spencer's in the shadows next to my bed, the shape of his body and head outlined yellow by the digital clock.

My ears are stuffed with earplugs, silicone ones that cut off the sounds of husbands who snore and children who talk in their sleep.

I dig one out of my ear and shift to my elbow.

"What's going on?" I say.

"My leg hurts," Spencer says.

I lean closer his way.

"What?" I say.

"My leg," he says. "It hurts."

My eyes burn and my head hurts.

I lie on the pillow again.

If I stay extra still and don't even breathe, he may turn out to be one of those out of body dreams where I imagine he's

here but he isn't. When I've been this tired, it's happened before; it could be happening now.

Spencer leans so close to my face, his stinky breath is up
my nose.

"Mom," he says, "wake up."

I push out of the covers and sit on the edge of the bed.

"Okay," I say, "okay, I'm awake."

The clock says 2:30 and that's just great. The baby was up
two hours ago, I've had about two hours of sleep, and now I'll
get maybe one more before the baby wakes up again.

Steve's on his side of the bed, breathing in and snoring out
and I want to shake him and say, "What's wrong with you,
sleeping over there, when Spencer is your job and the baby is
my job."

Instead, I look back to Spencer's shape in the night. I put
my feet on the floor and my arm around Spencer's shoulders.

"Come on," I whisper.

I move us into the hall and close the bedroom door. I get
Spencer past Josephine's nursery and down the hall to his
room without a sound. I close Spencer's door and his airport
rug is lit with the low glow of his night-light.

Together, we cross the runway and I tap his globe lamp
two times, the light going from low to high.

Spencer sits on the edge of his bed and he wears his Super-
man PJs, the big S inside a triangle on his chest and these blue
shorts that show his long white legs.

Part of me is still warm and sleepy in bed, but the other
part of me kneels and touches the cool skin of Spencer's leg.

"Where does it hurt?" I say.

"It's the other one," he says.

I move my hand to the other leg and touch down to his ankle and back up again. Spencer pulls away quick and his face goes light with a smile.

"You're tickling," he says.

I put my hand into my lap and there's no play in the sound of my voice.

"Spencer," I say, "it is late, where does it hurt?"

Spencer pulls his knee into his chest and hugs it tight.

"Mo-om," he says.

He drags the word out in that way that says I should magically know the source of his pain.

I put my finger to my lips.

"You're going to wake up the baby and Dad," I say.

Spencer stops and I rearrange him to lie flat on his bed.

For the last two months, Steve's been giving him his baths and getting him dressed for bed and I've been coming in after he's under the sheets and ready for a book.

Spencer's knees have changed and he's got a mess of bruises on his shins. I touch over the small collection of purple and brown spots.

"How did you get all these?" I say.

Spencer angles his head to see down where I touch, and he shrugs his shoulders like he doesn't know.

"Is that what hurts?" I say.

He shrugs again and I stand up.

On the side table, Spencer's globe lamp has the whole world drawn out with its continents, its seas, and the line for the equator.

A world of possibilities floats in my foggy head.

It's the bruises.

His leg fell asleep.

He's faking it, but I shake my head on that one. I'm sure I read something somewhere about how little kids don't fake pain.

Spencer is back up in his bed, his leg to his chest and he says, "Ow, ow, ow."

Since he was a baby, he's made some version of that sound, a cry at an octave that's tapped direct into my stomach, or maybe my heart, I don't know, but that sound turns off my thoughts, and calls me to action even when I don't have a clue what to do.

"Ow, ow, ow," he says and rocks at the same time.

I put my hands up.

"Hold on," I say, "stay right there."

In the bathroom I dig through the medicine cabinet for baby aspirins. On my way back to his room, I make it okay with myself to give him pills, since they can't really hurt him, and if this is a real pain, pills may help a little bit. At least I'm doing something.

In his room, he sits up on his bed, this look of real hope on his face.

I open my hand and two orange pills roll together in the center of my palm. Spencer pulls back like pills are the worst possible solution.

"Yuck," he says, "I hate those."

I close my fist and I am wide awake now.

"Goddammit, Spencer," I say. "I am trying to help you here. What is wrong with you?"

The words are fast and mad and they just snap out with that last-straw spark that we both know.

Spencer's eyes go round and his mouth is open.

I clear my throat and sit on the edge of his bed, trying not to be angry even though it's out there now.

"I'm sorry," I say, "but it's very late. Does your leg still hurt? Do you want to take these? What do you want?"

Spencer crosses his arms over himself, a pout on his face, and then he lets out this little fed-up sigh.

"I'll take them," he says.

I open my hand again and he takes the pills out of my palm and puts them into his mouth.

I get his water glass from the side table and hand it to him.

He drinks and I move his covers up over his legs.

He hands me the empty glass and I put it next to his globe lamp.

Spencer lies down, closes his eyes, and turns his back to me.

I lift his quilt closer over his shoulders, tucking him in, and I kiss him so light on the cheek I'm like air on his soft face.

Spencer keeps his eyes closed, not moving at all.

I touch the base of his globe lamp and turn off the world.

In our room, Steve is exactly like he was before. I move careful under the covers, barely moving the mattress. I lay my head on my pillow.

The clock reads 3:00 A.M. and Steve's breathing is deep on the inhale, gravel snore on the exhale. I work the earplugs deep into my ears and his snore turns into a quiet underwater sound.

I close my eyes, but in my head I see Spencer as he was when I left, this person who needed something who became a person who needed nothing. What did he really need? Why couldn't I give it to him?

I open my eyes again.

Before Spencer was born, I never asked questions like I do now. Before Spencer was born, I was never filled with so much doubt. Before Spencer was born, I slept like the dead.

One man I loved in my twenties was even jealous.

"You're so lucky you can sleep," he said.

Joshua was one of those people who never slept.

One night, we were together in his room watching *The Philadelphia Story*, that movie with Cary Grant, Jimmy Stewart, and Katharine Hepburn in a love triangle. Before the movie was halfway through, I passed out in Joshua's pillows.

When I woke, the TV in the bedroom was off and the covers were over me even though I didn't fall asleep that way.

It was three in the morning and there was a lift of light from Joshua's living room. I got out of bed, walked barefoot to the end of the hall, and leaned my shoulder into the wall. From where I stood, the mirror in the bathroom reflected the living room and Joshua bent over his drafting table. A retractable lamp was adjusted over the table, sending down a triangle of light over drafting paper.

He was sipping a glass of something on the rocks, and in his other hand he held one of those mechanical pencils. He put his drink on a coaster, the ice dancing against the glass, and took up an eraser, hunching his shoulders as he rubbed something off his page.

His day job was a TV news guy, but at night he drew these airliners of the future. They were beautiful too, like you'd see a professional do, with graceful fuselages, wide tapered wings, and cross-section renderings of turbo jet engines. He was so meticulous, he'd even draw the inside of his airliners, laying out the seats for first class and coach and sleeping berths for the crew, who would need to rest in the middle of their long-range flights.

Joshua set his eraser aside and went back to drawing a long, careful line.

Watching him there in his white bathrobe and slippers, I wasn't sure if he was a genius or just a tortured soul with demons who wouldn't let him rest. I hugged myself against his disease and went back to bed.

Then Spencer was born and just having him in the world shook something loose in me. He was my responsibility, he was my job, and with him came doubt and fear and dark nights when he'd call for food, for comfort, for healing, or just a clean set of sheets. After a while, I'd hear Spencer even when he didn't call for me and I was awake all the time.

I've read every book about how to sleep. I sipped relaxation teas and popped the herbal pills and pushed earplugs into my ears, always believing that my problem was something chemical or physical or that I just had to force myself to sleep. Except now, there's Josephine and she doesn't fill me with the fears and questions that I've always had with Spencer. Maybe it's because she's the second one and I know what to do. It could be the mystery of how one child is this way and the other is that way. No matter the reason, since she has been in my life, I've slept in peace. When she wakes up, I feed her and go back to sleep. With Spencer, it was never that way and it's not tonight. Something in him forces me to be awake and to think more deeply than I have ever thought before.

I roll my head on the pillow and the clock reads 3:30.

Outside is the sound of a car driving by, its headlights reflecting on the wall of our room, and I close my eyes.

When I was twelve, I went to live with my aunt and uncle in Nevada. They were big-boned, loud-mouthed people with a toddler of their own and they lived in a tiny box of a house near the state line. My uncle called me a "no-neck good-for-nothing kid" and yelled at me to get him extra packs of cigarettes and cups of coffee. My aunt would bounce their bald-headed baby on her wide knee and laugh out loud like he was so funny.

I was supposed to be adopted by these people and they were going to change my name. There was a problem though, they weren't anything like me and I didn't feel the love you should feel when you are going to be part of a family. Was it me who didn't love them or was it the other way around? I didn't know, but I couldn't get right with the idea that I was going to become one of them without knowing the answer.

I was in bed one night and I figured it was time to put them to the test.

It was hot the way it got in Nevada in the summer, that ticking heat where the air snaps over the ground. It was even ticking in the quiet of their house as I lay on the bottom bunk of their bunk bed set. I rolled myself right out of bed and slapped my body on the floor the way you might if you fell out of bed and were fast asleep.

The floor was cold linoleum and when I hit, my bones hurt and there were lights in my head.

I lay still and quiet, waiting for one of them to wake up and run to my rescue.

The house ticked.

I slapped my hands on the floor, a loud clap of a sound.

Nothing.

I rolled on my back and thought about pulling covers and a pillow down with me. I could just sleep there on the floor, and in the morning they'd wake up to find me that way and maybe feel bad the way people did when they really cared.

I smacked my hands on the floor again and down the hall, their door was open. How could they not hear me?

If it was my mother or father, I know they'd be up. I could almost see my father running to my room, I could feel him pick me up with his long, strong arms and tuck me safe between my sheets while he said something like, "You are so silly, how did that happen?"

I got up then, shaking dust bunnies off my nightgown, and walked down the hall.

Their room was so small, the only thing that fit in there was a mattress butted next to a dresser. On the bed, my uncle was on his back, the sheets barely over his leg and chest, his big-boned self hogging the whole bed, and my aunt was in a ball in the corner, making herself small even though that was impossible.

They snored together, this stereo sound of strangers who didn't tune in to me and probably never would. They weren't my mother and father and even after they adopted me, they wouldn't be my mother and father, not the way I needed them to be.

Maybe it was not having a mother and father anymore that made me sad, or maybe the sadness was something that had been in my soul for a million years, waiting for the right time to cry it all out. I don't know, but that night I didn't know how to wake those people up and say, "Help me find the way."

I walked back down the hall, closed the door of my room, climbed into the bottom bunk, and rolled on my side with my back to the rest of the house.

I went to sleep that night and I've been sleeping ever since, or at least until now, until Spencer.

When I wake up the next morning, Steve is gone. The clock says 9:00 A.M. and I haven't slept this late since before Spencer was born.

I lie under my earplugs and blink awake. Between the shades on the windows, there are slices of bright sunlight.

I dig an earplug from my ear, take out the other one, and stretch out long.

It doesn't take long for me to think myself back to where I left off the night before, but with rest and daylight the whole thing is different.

Spencer probably didn't have a sore leg, but he did need something and didn't know how to ask.

Isn't that what happens to us in our lives? Don't we all reach out in our nights and our days, full of some mysterious agenda, and hope another person can somehow read our minds and give us our heart's desire? I wonder why we are like this. What happens to us along the way that makes us so afraid to ask for what we really want? And what do we become when we lose that ability? I know I've become one of the people who never asks for help, who can't even imagine it, but is that the way I want Spencer to be?

Some questions take a lifetime to answer.

Out of bed, I put on my robe and go downstairs.

In the living room, Josephine is cradled in Steve's arm while he sits on the floor with Spencer. Lego blocks are in a mountain between them and Spencer builds something with a propeller. Steve gives Jo a square block to hold in her hand.

He looks my way and smiles one of his best smiles that sends a shimmer of light into his blue eyes.

"You're up," Steve says.

Spencer turns fast.

"MOM," he yells.

He drops his machine and jumps up. He runs to where I am and puts his arms around my waist.

I put my arm around him, winding it down his back and around his waist.

"Hey, you," I say, "how are you feeling this morning?"

"Better," Spencer says.

Josephine follows the sound of us and she grins so big, it lifts into her blue eyes.

Spencer's wrapped against my side and I walk this funny limp walk that gets us to the sofa.

"Spencer told me he woke up last night," Steve says. "What was wrong?"

"I have no idea," I say, sitting down. "He said his leg was sore and I gave him two baby aspirins."

"Do you think it was a growing pain?" Steve says.

"Maybe," I say, "or a cramp."

Spencer noodles in closer to me, and takes up a piece of my hair. He winds it tight around his finger, the tip turning white.

"Mom," he says, "I'm sorry I woke you up and you got mad at me."

I move my hand over Spencer's head.

"I did get mad, didn't I?"

"You yelled," Spencer says.

"I did yell," I say.

He lets my hair go through his finger and takes up another piece.

"That wasn't very nice," I say. "I am such a grouch when I'm tired."

Spencer nods like he knows.

"I told Spencer he needs to wake me up," Steve says, "at least until the baby is sleeping all the way through the night."

Josephine makes a sputter sound and her eyes take in everything: Spencer, me, Steve, the Legos.

I move Spencer onto my lap and hold him like I held him when he was a baby, except he doesn't quite fit.

"Is that okay with you?" I say. "Can you wake up Dad and let Mom get some sleep?"

"It's okay," Spencer says.

I take Spencer's leg at the knee and lift it up so his shin is close to my face.

"You, Mr. Crazy Leg, you need to stop waking Spencer up," I say.

Spencer laughs at this, a giggle that makes his eyes squint.

"It's the other leg, Mom," he says.

I let his leg go and pick up the other one.

"You're the crazy leg," I say. "Now enough, let the boy sleep."

Spencer twists and turns and laughs so hard he spills off my lap.

I follow him down to the floor and tickle all his spots, under the arms, in the hollow under his knees, and at his waist.

"Break," he yells, "break."

I stop and sit back on my heels to readjust my robe and tighten the belt around my waist.

On Steve's lap, Josephine smiles and claps her little hands together like she can't wait to be big enough to get in on the fun.

# CHILD ABUSE AWARENESS WEEK

"Are you ready?" I said.

Spencer pulled his scuba mask down to fit tight under his nose. The plastic wedged in and puckered his top lip out.

"Ready," he said.

I tossed the keys in the air, but instead of throwing them into the water, I let them drop back into my palm.

"Are you sure?" I said.

"Mo-ooom!"

He whined delicious agony. Spencer loved this kind of game.

"Okay," I said. "Here goes."

I let the keys fly and they arced low to the surface to splash in the center of the pool. Water rings spread out and Spencer's slim body lifted like a fish. His stomach pulled in with a deep inhale of breath, his ribs pressed against his skin, and he dove under to where I couldn't see him anymore.

It was a Wednesday afternoon and we had the little

hot pool to ourselves. It was a public place, but it was tucked in the courtyard of an old elementary school. Spencer and I knew the secret of how no one ever came here before three in the afternoon.

A wrought-iron fence ran along one side, and on the other there was the brick wall of the school. Evergreen trees and bushes surrounded us and some of the bushes bloomed with tiny white flowers that filled the courtyard with a thick, sweet smell.

Spencer exploded to the surface of the water, the keys in his fist.

I clapped my hands and the sound chased itself around the courtyard.

He dog-paddled to where I sat, stopping a little short, and tossed the keys my way. I reached up and caught them in my palm.

"Do it again," he said.

I threw the keys six, ten, twenty times and the wind blew against the brick wall, churning the steam into a dance over the water.

When Spencer was finally tired out, we rested in the shallow water of the steps, spread out in this way that let him put his head in the soft of my arm.

I read somewhere that from the very beginning women floated in everything from the rivers to the sea, with faces to the sky as their children held the lifelines of their hair. I didn't know if it was true, but it was a good story since being at the pool was one of my favorite things to do with Spencer.

"I see an ice-cream cone," he said.

"Right there?" I said.

He poked at the sky with one definite finger.

"No, there," he said.

Spencer drew a wide circle with his hand.

"And that's a fire truck," he said.

"Where?" I said.

"Right there," he said.

"Got it," I said. "Okay, a fire truck."

Spencer shook his head like I had it all wrong.

"It's not anymore, Mom," he said, "it's a duck now."

"Hmm," I said, "a duck, okay."

I was still pregnant with Josephine then, at the last stage where I was almost uncomfortable, and while we looked at the sky, there was a deep push from inside followed by two quick jabs.

"She's kicking," I said, "or punching."

I moved Spencer's hand just north of my belly button.

"Feel it?" I said.

Spencer stayed very still and when the next hit came, he pulled his hand away.

"Isn't that weird?" I said.

He didn't say if it was weird or not, he just looked at the sky again. His silence filled me with the noise of questions. When will she finally get here, and when she comes, how will it all go, how will Spencer change, how will I change?

Spencer had his face to the clouds and I wondered if a million questions were burning through his head too.

Spencer rolled his head on the pillow of my arm.

"I'm starving," he said.

I looked at him and he looked at me and then I laughed out loud. He'd never said the word "starving" before.

"Starving?" I said.

"It was the word of the day at school."

"Are you really starving or did you just want to use the word?"

Spencer went serious and nodded.

"I'm really starving," he said.

I shrugged my shoulder under his head, jogging him a little.

"Okay," I said, "let's go eat."


When Josephine arrived, life went on its usual way. Spencer was in school and I was at my computer checking e-mail messages.

*A girl! We are so happy for you!*

*9 pounds, 8 ounces?!! Can you still walk?*

*Josephine! What a beautiful name.*

I scroll down the incoming mail and the baby is asleep in a vibrating chair that I've put on the desk, right next to the computer monitor. In the reflection of the screen, I see myself in a bathrobe and a towel wrapped around my head. I answer the congratulations with a photo of her, since it's never too soon to start boring my friends with the endless run of pictures and little notes that proclaim that my mound of baby flesh that looks exactly like everyone else's mound is actually the most beautiful. I think that's called bonding anyway, and I do it with abandon. After all, it's true. My Josephine is the most beautiful baby in the universe.

The motor of the chair vibrates the desk, the keyboard, and the mouse as she sleeps with her head tucked to her chin. The corner of the blanket is over the edge of the seat and I tuck it tight around her feet.

The last incoming e-mail is a note of congratulations attached to a plea.

*Come speak for us next month, we need you.*

I can see this friend in my mind. Klaus Scherler, journalism advisor and writer, both a friend and a former teacher from a community college in Spokane. I've known Klaus for at least twenty years.

Back in the eighties, he was the perfect profile of my perfect man: tall, handsome, and old enough to be my dad. What could have been never was. I was in the thick of my first marriage and he was married with a child. Instead, that spark between us became great teaching and great learning.

*The subject,* Klaus writes, *is child abuse awareness and I know you're going to say that you don't have the authority to talk about this, but you do, you lived child abuse, you wrote about it in your books and besides, I've seen you speak. People would watch you read a shopping list.*

I laugh out loud. Klaus always was a man who could flatter a girl, and honestly, I could use a little flattery. Here I sit post-baby, and I'm soft, out of shape, and tired. A little Internet flirting is exactly what I need.

I put my hands to the keyboard and the sound of my fingers is steady raindrops beating down on plastic.

I write: *Thanks Klaus, but you've got to be kidding. The baby is just a few weeks old, I'm wiped out, and overwhelmed with the house and Spencer . . .*

I stop typing and sit back in my chair.

My words on the page read flat. The truth is, I'd really like to go. I'd like to see Klaus, I'd love to help him out, and I'd even be happy to live up to his expectation of me.

Next to the desk is a window and out that window is a hedge with bright green bushes. March rain puddles on the surface of the fat leaves and streams over the edges, making a natural waterfall.

Is a terrible childhood enough to give me a voice? Could I say something, anything, that would make a difference? If I don't try, the answer will be no, but if I do try, the answer could be yes.

I sit up tall in my chair again. I backspace my words away to *Thanks Klaus*. Even though I have no idea what I will talk about and I don't know where I'll find the time to compose a speech, I write a new message.

*Tell me the date and I'll be there.*


A couple weeks later, I stand at the top of the landing and call down the basement steps.

"Come on, Spence," I say, "let's get going."

Spencer is at the bottom landing and he holds his empty hands open.

"Mom," he says, "I can't find it anywhere."

The time on my watch reads 3:30.

"We have to go, Spence," I say, "if we don't go, too many people will be at the pool."

"I can't go without my mask," he says.

The baby cries and Slavka bounces her up and down in her arm, speaking adorations and questions in her broken English.

"No, no cry, my baby, my beautiful girl," she says. "You hungry? You no want your momma to go?"

I love Slavka, she helped me with Spencer and now is helping with Jo, but she has a way of making it hard to get out of the house when I need to leave.

I back away from both baby and Slavka, but Josephine's cry taps direct into my nervous system and my breasts go hard with a fresh supply of milk.

I wave Spencer to come up.

"Forget the mask, let's go."

"Mom," Spencer says, "we have to find it first."

I put my hands over my breasts, as if that's going to stop nature.

"No," I say, "come, come, we are so late."

Josephine cries louder, and Spencer bursts into tears too.

"I don't want to go swimming," he cries.

I keep ahold of my breasts and nod at Slavka.

"She'll be fine," I say, "just feed her the bottle on the counter and we'll be back in a couple hours."

I kiss the baby on her forehead and make myself walk away. Spencer's there with his arms crossed tight over himself.

"I don't want to go swimming," he says.

I grab our swim bag and the keys off the counter.

"Fine," I say, "I'm going. You can stay here with Slavka."

"No-ooooo," he howls. "Don't leave me."

"Well, come on then," I say.

He's up the steps that fast and I usher him to the door with a hand between his shoulder blades.

"Bye, Slavka," I say.

Over the sound of Josephine's cries, Slavka says, "Bye-bye."

By the time we are changed and into the pool, it's well past four in the afternoon and the secret is out. There are mothers and kids who take up all the room on the steps, a couple who makes out in the corner, and three women who sit together reading fashion magazines.

Spencer complains that it's too hot, that he's tired and hungry, that he wants to go home. In the water, I float to where he sits at the pool edge and I jangle our keys.

"Do you want to dive for these?" I say.

"No," he says.

He kicks water in the direction of the lovebirds and I put my hands on his knees.

"Spencer," I say, "don't splash, be considerate."

I put our keys down next to him and hold my hands open.

"Come on," I say, "I'll give you a piggyback."

Spencer shakes his head but won't speak.

I put my hands on his ankles.

"Honey, please," I say, "we don't get much time to be together. Let's play. Let's have fun."

Spencer shakes his head again and kicks water into my face.

Once when Spencer was still a baby, we took our regular walk around the neighborhood. I had him in his kangaroo carrier, his chest snuggled against mine, and I had my hands together around his back.

The neighborhood was quiet the way it got in the middle of the day when people were at work and kids were at school. We went past houses with empty front yards and porch swings, but then came to a front yard that wasn't empty. Out front, there was a tricycle, a bicycle with training wheels, a plastic playhouse, and a bunch of other plastic toys.

From the shadows of the front porch came the high yell of a woman. She had this caw sound in her voice, like a big crow makes while it's fighting for its fair share of roadkill.

I kept walking, trying not to look, but looking anyway from the side of my eye.

The woman with the voice was on the front steps with her little girl and the little girl had her hands on her hips.

"Don't talk back to me," the woman yelled. She grabbed the girl by what could have been her hair or her ear, I couldn't tell, and yanked her up the steps. The little girl stumbled and made this horrible sound that was a scream mixed with a cry. She fought against the woman, pulling at her arms to get away, but she was too small.

I didn't realize I stopped walking but I did.

There was more screaming, more pulling, and the girl tripped up the steps. Then they were in the house and the door slammed shut. The screams went on from inside, but it wasn't as loud.

My hands were at my sides, my feet were planted solid on the sidewalk, and everything in me wanted to cross the street and say something like, "Take it easy, cool off, give yourself a time-out."

Then the house went completely quiet and it was just me on the sidewalk with my baby and the sunshine.

A hot wind blew in my face and my mouth was dry. I put one foot in front of the other and walked again.

The afternoon sun was high in the sky and it made the shadows of the trees fall long over the sidewalk. My feet moved from light to shadow and back to light again. Why didn't I do anything and did not doing anything make me a bad person.

I turned the corner and walked the block to our house where there were no trees to protect us from the direct sun.

I moved my hands together to shade Spencer and I couldn't stop thinking about the woman and the little girl. The only comfort I finally found for myself was in making a promise to Spencer.

"Don't you worry, little boy," I said, "I will never be like that."

After Spencer kicks water in my face, I'm done with the pool. We get out, get dressed and head out to the parking lot with me walking fast and Spencer dragging behind.

I adjust the strap of the swim bag over my shoulder. Wet towels and bathing suits soak into my back through the canvas of the bag and I jiggle my car keys, pushing the button that automatically unlocks the doors.

Twenty paces back, Spencer kicks at nothing on the sidewalk.

"Darn it, Spencer," I say, "come on."

Spencer walks a beat slower, his chin to his chest.

At the car, I open his door and everything about the way I wait is pissed off.

From inside the car, the cell phone rings, but I have a rule about that. When I'm with someone else, I never answer the telephone. It's just so rude. It says, "You're interesting, but this call is probably more interesting," and the only time I break the rule is for emergencies. Today though, anything is more interesting than Spencer. I grab it on the third ring.

On the phone is a woman who works for a newspaper in Spokane and she wants to ask a few questions for an article she's writing.

"We're doing a story about the Child Abuse Awareness speech you're giving at the college."

"Oh, hi," I say.

In my voice there's a fake sound that comes from the fact that I haven't even thought about the speech yet.

"So what will you be talking about?" she says. "What's the theme?"

"The theme?" I say. "Hmm, that's a good question."

Spencer stalls at the curb and I balance the telephone between ear and shoulder, lifting him off his feet.

"Well, of course, it's child abuse," I say.

I carry him to the car but he's so heavy, I can barely lift him and talk at the same time.

"And I'll be talking about it," I grunt.

I get him into the car and pull the seat belt over his lap.

"I'm starving," he says.

I point to the telephone in our code that says, "Don't interrupt Mommy on the telephone."

"I'll read from my book and talk about the effects of abuse based on my own experience," I say, "and there will be other things."

I make sure his feet and hands are tucked in safe and I shut his door.

The reporter on the line doesn't say anything and I know I'm not making a lot of sense, even to myself. I should tell her that I will call her back, but I stumble ahead, trying to sound like I know what the hell I'm talking about.

"I'm hungry," Spencer says.

I start up the car and back it up, giving Spencer another one of my "don't interrupt me" looks.

"I WANT SOMETHING TO EAT," Spencer yells just as the reporter asks a question, which, of course, I cannot hear.

I put my foot on the break and stop the car hard.

"Can you hold one minute, please?" I say.

"Of course," the reporter says.

I put my hand over the receiver and look Spencer dead on.

"Do you want me to leave you here?" I say. "Because I will. I will just open the door and you can get out."

I shake a finger at him for added effect.

Spencer goes silent and his eyes are these merciless magnets that never seem to take a break.

I turn in my seat and take my hand off the receiver.

"I apologize," I say, "it's always when you're on the phone, isn't it?"

The reporter laughs and it's like we share a joke.

"I know," she says, "I have two kids, they make you crazy sometimes."

"You're not kidding," I say.

She starts up where we left off, but I don't hear her voice anymore and the shared joke isn't that funny. I read somewhere that children actually know when their mother isn't focused on them, that it has to do with the chemistry between mother and child and that it's instinct for kids to try to get their mother's attention, as a course of survival. How can I joke about something that is primal in my child and worse, how can it be okay to yell at him for it?

In my head, I hear the sound of my own voice as I was yelling and it was this shrill, mean sound, like a crow. I can't believe I made that terrible sound. Worse, I can't believe I said such a terrible thing, especially since I know that being left behind is a kid's worst fear.

I turn around and Spencer's face is white, like he's freezing cold, and he's so small back there.

"Look," I say, "can I call you back in a little while, after I get home?"

The reporter says that's fine and I snap the telephone shut.

I pull the car back into the parking spot and shift into park.

I turn around in my seat and put my hand over my heart.

"I am so sorry I said that to you," I say.

Spencer crosses his arms against me and his bottom lip tries so hard to hold on.

"Would you leave me?" he says.

I reach between the seat and hold his small round knee.

"No," I say, "never, ever, ever."

His lip gives way to full-on, brokenhearted-kid crying that ruins me completely.

"Oh, Spencer," I say.

I crawl between the seats to wedge myself into the back. I undo Spencer's seat belt and pull him onto my lap.

"I'm so sorry," I say, using the sleeve of my shirt to wipe his nose. "Mom really screwed that up."

I try to explain that I'm tired and grouchy, and how things are just different now with Josephine in our world.

Spencer's down to just a sniff or two and his body is all warm in my arms. I press into the warm smell of him and his dark hair is wet and cool against my face.

"You okay?" I say.

Spencer nods like, "Yeah, I'm okay," but the way he stays still, I know he's not going to crawl out of my lap anytime soon.

We sit like that for the longest time and I have to laugh to myself. Here I am, trying to talk about child abuse as I, in a way, abuse my own kid. Talk about ironic. I can just see the headline now. "Abusive Mother Speaks at Alma Mater." Klaus would be dazzled.

I rock Spencer on my lap, the two of us all warm and cud-dly in the car, and I don't think I've done permanent damage, but I know I crossed a line. The only thing I can do now is say I'm sorry and explain to Spencer that I make mistakes.

Spencer has wet eyes and I dab at them with my sleeve.

"I think we were both pretty grumpy today," I say.

Spencer nods against my chest.

"That's okay," he says, "that's normal."

"That's true, Spencer," I say. "People get mad and that's normal."

"But it's not good to hurt feelings," he says.

"That's right," I say. "But when you do, you say you're sorry, right?"

"Right," he says.

He looks up at me and his eyes are so big and round, I could tip right over and fall into them.

"I'm sorry, Mom," he says.

"I'm sorry too, Spencer," I say.

He hugs around my neck then, holding on tight, and it's not swimming or looking at the clouds, but it's something.

I kiss over his cheeks and smile at him. Spencer grins back and it takes away the sadness in his eyes.

"I'm starved," he says.

I laugh out loud, but he doesn't laugh, Spencer's always se-rious when it comes to food.

"Okay," I say. "Let's go home and we'll get something to eat."

# ON DRUGS

Spencer sat on my lap and I rocked him in the pendulum of a clock motion. He pressed his ear against my heart and I held my hand over the other ear that was hot under my palm. Usually, hot ears meant Spencer was tired, but he was hot all over with a fever too.

We were at the doctor's office and had made it through the gauntlet of scheduling the appointment, checking in with a receptionist, producing the insurance card to be copied, paying our copay, and sitting in the waiting room with all the other sickies. Now we were in the examining room, another twenty minutes had gone by, and any minute, the doctor would appear.

I prayed he would appear.

I even willed him through the door.

Spencer coughed and the sound jump-started my own cough. I put my fist to my mouth and we both shook.

I dug into my jacket pocket for a pack of travel tissues and pulled out one for Spencer and another for myself. I set him back a little and covered his nose.

"Here," I said. "Blow."

He honked out a hunk of snot and I mopped around his nose. I wiped at my own nose and pushed both tissues back into my pocket.

Spencer curved into my chest and we went back to rocking.

The closed door of our room was decorated with a poster of a giant ear. It showed the outer ear, the middle ear, the inner ear, and all the technical words that go with the universe of the ear: eustachian tube. Cochlear canal. Basilar membrane. I wasn't here to be a student of the ear though, I was here acting calm in all the waiting, but my act was a cover. I wanted, no, needed, the doctor to get into the room and make my son well again.

There was a knock on the door and Dr. Green was there with his beard in need of a trim, wire-rimmed glasses smeared with fingerprints, and a tie with zebras who peeked from behind dark green grass. No man ever looked so good to me.

Through the phlegm and misery and exhaustion, my body was flooded with a warm wave of relief. I wanted to say, "Thank God, you're finally here," but instead held Spencer that much tighter in my arms, sat up a little more in my chair, and grinned at Dr. Green.

"Hiya, Spencer," Dr. Green said.

Spencer lifted a hand like "hello" and let it fall down again.

"Hi, Jennifer," Dr. Green said.

"Hi, Dr. Green," I said.

Dr. Green closed the door and held a manila file under his arm.

"How are you guys doing?" he said.

Like Dr. Green, I had on my glasses, the ones that were crooked on my face ever since Spencer sat on them. I adjusted the glasses to be straight.

"Not so good," I said. "This guy coughed all night."

Dr. Green put Spencer's file on the counter and turned on the taps to wash his hands.

"Did you use a humidifier?"

"Yes I did," I said, "and cough syrup and cough drops and that menthol stuff you smear on his chest."

Dr. Green turned the water off and pulled a paper towel from the dispenser.

"No good, huh?" he said.

"No good," I said.

Spencer sneezed and his nose ran green down to his lip. I pulled out more tissues.

"I'm pretty sure it's in his ears again," I said.

Dr. Green pulled a stool from under the examining table.

"Let's take a look."

Spencer was three that year and by then I knew this part of the drill. I'd put Spencer on the table, Dr. Green would get out a mini flashlight to look down his throat and then into his ears. He'd say, "Yep, he's got some blistering in there," scribble "amoxicillin" on a pad, hand me the sheet of paper, saying, "This should do the trick."

Spencer was almost two years old the first time I got that sheet of paper and it wasn't just an antibiotic, it was a miracle pink goo I squirted down Spencer's throat three times a day for a week. It was easy, it tasted great, and Spencer got better fast. Then, there was another cold, another infection, another run of antibiotics. Six ear infections later, it wasn't such a miracle anymore.

Dr. Green kept one eye closed while he looked into Spencer's ear with his funnel flashlight.

"Yep," Dr. Green said, "he's got some blistering in there."

He snapped the light off, scooted himself across the room on the stool, and pulled open a drawer.

Spencer's legs hung over the edge of the table, his chin tucked to his chest and he leaned his weight into me.

"I don't understand why his colds keep turning into infections," I said.

Dr. Green took out a pad of paper and while he wrote, nodded at the big ear poster.

"It has to do with the maturity of the eustachian tube," he said. "Children's ears have a way of collecting fluid . . ."

I'd heard this story so many times that I zoned out on his words until they stopped at,

". . . should grow out of it," Dr. Green said.

"I know all that," I said, "I just don't understand why he gets an infection with every cold. It just doesn't make sense. I wonder if I should do something, like try some herbs or vitamin C, or maybe some health food?"

As fast I zoned him out, Dr. Green zoned me out and shook his head before I finished.

"There's nothing conclusive about the effects of herbs or vitamins," he said, "and his diet shouldn't make a difference either."

I looked down at my own feet on the floor and my glasses slid down my nose. The floor was crooked through them and I set them higher on my nose again, thinking there had to be a connection between all the antibiotics and Spencer's endless infections, but then again, what did I know? I didn't go to medical school and I wasn't a doctor. What if I was wrong and Spencer got worse?

There was a thick glob of junk in my throat and I swallowed it down. Spencer coughed again and I dug into my pocket for the pack that was empty. I pulled out an old tissue instead, his, mine, I was past caring.

"If he doesn't get better, call us," Dr. Green said, "but this should do the trick."

He put the sheet of paper on the counter, tucked Spencer's file under his arm, and got up.

"Take care of your mom, Spencer," Dr. Green said and he winked at me.

Spencer sniffed and made this half smile.

"Thanks, Dr. Green," I said.

Dr. Green left then and I coughed so hard, my glasses almost fell off. I caught them quick and stood there with my arm around Spencer's hot shoulders.

Alone in the examining room again, there was this stomped down feeling in the center of my chest, maybe disappointment, maybe disillusionment.

I cleared my throat and pulled Spencer into my arms, a wet rag of a child who draped heavy on my chest.

Even though I was the big one, the mother, I wasn't that much different from Spencer. I felt just like a little kid, I felt lost. I had come to Dr. Green in search of answers, in search of a cure, in search of expertise that surpassed my own but was leaving with a slip of paper that wasn't any of those things.

Spencer pressed his hot face into the side of my neck.

"I'm tired, Mommy," he said.

I rubbed over his back.

"I know," I said, "let's get you home."

I took the prescription off the counter, wadded it in my hand, and shoved it into my pocket with the dirty tissues.

A month later, I lay on one of those plastic mattresses you blow up with a foot pump and it was the guest bed in Rebecca's extra bedroom. She had put a set of sheets on the mattress, but there was no pad underneath and the plastic never got warm.

Rebecca was an old friend from Portland who had moved to L.A. I was there for work and Rebecca was letting me crash at her place. She had no idea I was sick and I had no plans to tell her.

My stomach turned on itself, this deep, twisting tug, and I pulled my knees into my chest, the plastic of the bed moving under me. I held on tight and it was better that way, like my body couldn't argue for a little while.

From a narrow slice of window, a rectangle of sunlight angled into the room. Outside there was some blue sky, the dirt gray of L.A. fog, and the sway of a palm leaf against the glass.

Black memories hung in the smoggy air. I hated this city and being sick here made me hate it that much more. My mother was sick here and died at the UCLA Medical Center, my father had his heart attack here and died in a hospital in Orange County. I was close to homeless here and was molested here. Whenever I came here, I wondered why the hell I was here again.

I was here though and, almost out of spite, I wasn't going to give in to whatever was wrong with me. I had bullied my way through being sick before and I could do it again.

Twelve hours later though, I lost the fight.

We were in Rebecca's little sports car, driving back to Los

Angeles after dinner in Long Beach, and the freeway was thick
with six lanes of fast cars. There were so many headlights, it
looked like the stars were on the ground.

"You should have told me you were sick," Rebecca said.
"We didn't have to come all the way down here."

Rebecca's little-girl face and curly dark hair were backlit by
the headlights of a passing car.

"I didn't want to spoil our time together," I said.

Rebecca shook her head the way she did when she was irritated.

In the quiet of the car, headlights sent shadows over the
dashboard, my legs, and then they slid away to leave the car
dark.

Rebecca nodded my way.

"So what's wrong?" she said.

I adjusted the seat up to see to the freeway over the top of
her dashboard.

"I don't know," I said, "I'm on this antibiotic for an infection and I think I'm allergic to it or something."

"Yuck," she said.

I hugged around my stomach and held on.

"Tell me about it," I said. "I'm all bloated and it's like I
have to go to the bathroom, but can't. It's awful."

"I hope you stopped taking them," she said.

"I did," I said.

Rebecca put her signal on and got into the fast lane.

Just being with her and talking about it made me feel better somehow. It made me remember how much I liked Rebecca. She was the oldest daughter of a doctor, but was also
this free-spirit career girl who had never been married and

didn't have any kids. She was an alternative health person too, she ate pure food, did acupuncture, and took a whole cache of vitamins. She was that way when she lived in Portland and now, living in Los Angeles, she was in the middle of health nut heaven. Here, it was tofu this and wheat grass that and Rebecca said she even had something called a life coach.

I laughed out loud when she told me that. "What the hell is a life coach?"

"Don't laugh," Rebecca said, "she's great, she's like a therapist and a friend all wrapped up into one package."

There was something about Rebecca's whole thing that kept me at a distance though. Something about her tripped a memory of my stepmother, who wasn't just high on the L.A. alternative lifestyle, she was a junkie who had joined this cult where people stared at each other for hours and tried to bend spoons with the power of their minds. In the middle of all this, my stepmother went on a health food kick where we drank goat's milk and took a mountain of vitamins for everything. I remember taking a thick white pill that even made you stop farting.

We were quiet in the car and out a ways, there was a factory or a refinery with a flame that burned at the top of a high, narrow stack.

"What is that fire?" I said.

Rebecca lifted her chin and squinted.

"I have no idea," she said.

The flame licked at the sky and there were other towers too, at least a dozen of them shooting dense white and gray smoke to the sky. The towers were part of this metal maze that looked like a kid's erector set and it was all lit up with brilliant yellow floodlights as if to say, "I have nothing to hide."

"You'd think there'd be some environmentalists going crazy about all that smoke and that flame," I said, "it can't be safe."

Rebecca frowned.

"It has to be safe," she said, "they wouldn't be able to burn it like that if it wasn't."

"They who?" I said.

"You know," she said, "the people in charge of the place."

She looked again, but didn't say anything, and then she looked over at her blind spot and pulled out of the fast lane.

Around us, other cars passed and no one seemed to notice the flame or the smoke. Everyone was in their own world, talking, laughing, sleeping, or just staring straight ahead.

"You know," Rebecca said, "you should see a naturopath or a nutritionist."

I shifted my eyes off the flame and to the dark inside the car. The only light was on her dashboard that showed the speedometer and all her gauges and knobs.

"At least talk to someone who can help get your immune system strong enough that you don't need antibiotics," she said.

The freeway had a bunch of interchanges with twists and turns of lanes that took cars away. We passed the factory and the interchanges and the freeway opened up with half as many cars.

"I know a bunch of people in Portland," she said, "I can check my Rolodex, make a few calls, you know, network."

"For what?" I said. "A life coach?"

She laughed and waved her hand at me.

"Ha ha," she said. "No, a nutritionist."

My stomach bubbled deep from my core and I looked out the window at the dark of the night.

"I know what you meant," I said, "I was just kidding."

*          *          *

Back in Portland, I found my own sweet-smiling nutritionist, herbalist, and registered nurse named Maria Elena something and something else. Her name was longer than her title and I couldn't get past the Maria Elena part anyway.

After a talk with Maria Elena, she had me convinced that I needed to be flat on my back on a table that had a hole near my behind and a plastic tube pushed inside a place that was supposed to be for exits, not entrances.

I was dressed from the waist up, but not from the waist down, and there was a thick white towel over me for privacy.

"Now just relax," Maria Elena said.

I laughed out loud and my sound filled the small room.

"Right," I said, "this is definitely the kind of position I get in when I want to relax."

Maria Elena didn't laugh, but she nodded like she knew. Even though the whole thing was strange, there was something about Maria Elena that was soft and kind, maybe it was her big brown eyes or her gentle voice, but I believed she was going to show me something I needed to know.

"You're doing fine," Maria Elena said.

She turned two faucets marked hot and cold and I heard the sound of water.

I held my hands on my stomach and it filled like a water bed.

"Are you okay?" Maria Elena said. "Is the temperature good?"

I nodded like, "Sure, this is dandy."

Soft music played from speakers overhead, flutes mixed with waterfalls, and the lights were dim. Maria Elena pushed her thumbs into my insteps while we waited for the water to come back the other way. The massage helped me relax a little, not much, but a little.

Behind her was a diagram of the human body from the inside out, mostly of the intestines.

"Where will the water go?" I said.

Maria Elena nodded over her shoulder at the diagram.

"The lower intestine," she said. "You'll know when you're full because you'll feel like you have to push."

To my right and down a ways, there was a wide transparent tube and it made me think of an aquarium where fish swam on the other side of the glass, only fish wouldn't be swimming there. At least, I hoped not.

I held my hands flat over my stomach and there was that unmistakable call-of-nature feeling.

"I feel it," I said.

Maria Elena smiled like she was so happy for me.

"Go ahead," she said.

At first I couldn't and I laughed out loud.

"I can't tell you how weird this is," I said.

"It's totally normal," Maria Elena said, "just relax."

I took a deep breath.

"Relax," I said, "okay, I'm relaxing."

Nothing happened, and I had to turn inside and say, Jennifer, she is a nurse, you have pushed a baby into the world, for heaven's sake, just push already.

I took another deep breath and pushed.

Maria Elena stopped rubbing my feet and came to my side, adjusting the water and pressing a couple of buttons with timers attached to them.

"Here we go," she said.

There were a whole series of stages that came next. There was the Oh my God, I can't believe I'm doing this stage, the What the hell is that floating by stage, the Jeez, look at all the crap inside of me stage, and then, the clear water with tiny grains of couscous floating around stage.

"That is yeast," Maria Elena said.

I wouldn't know a yeast if it hit me in the face and I squinted at the stuff floating in the water.

"Is that bad?" I said.

"Not if you have a little yeast," she said. "That's not a little yeast, that's a lot of yeast."

"They look big," I said.

She nodded.

"They are," she said, "they've been living the good life for quite some time now. Some of them are very mature."

I tried to see what Maria Elena saw, except I couldn't. It was just a mass of wheat-colored stuff floating around.

"How did they get so big?" I said.

Maria Elena smiled down at me.

"Do you eat a lot of sugar?"

"Some."

"Bread?"

"Yeah."

"Drink alcohol?"

I nodded yes, of course, yes to everything.

"You're talking my daily diet here," I said.

"There you go," she said, "that's the fuel for yeast."

It was like a car accident I couldn't look away from, I was stuck on the view of my insides on the outside, the water running clear except for little leftover pellets of yeast that wouldn't quit.

Maria Elena talked then, said the yeast came from taking a lot of antibiotics. She said the drugs killed bad bacteria, but they killed good bacteria too, which is what you needed in your intestines to keep yeast and parasites under control. She said a lot of traditional doctors didn't tell patients about this side effect.

"And it's so simple too," she said, "all you need is a little acidophilus while you take the drugs, or even an antiyeast medication to go with them."

Some beeper went off and Maria Elena turned the nozzles until they were all the way off, her hands moving with the skill of someone who has turned the knobs many times.

The last bit of the water drained away and I was so tired, I could have gone right to sleep.

Maria Elena put a hand on my shoulder

"Just rest for a minute and then get dressed," Maria Elena said. "I'll meet you in my office when you're ready."

She left me then and the only sound was the flutes, the waterfalls, and the drip of the water out of me that was finally crystal clear.

I found Maria Elena in her office and she was writing on a yellow pad of legal paper.

"Come on in and sit," she said.

I sat in a stiff chair by her desk and held my purse in my lap.

She went back to writing.

"Cut out sugar and anything with yeast for at least two weeks," she said. "Go to the natural grocery store and get a yeast cleanse for yourself and some acidophilus for your son."

"No sugar?" I said. "Really?"

She stopped writing and put her brown eyes on me.

"Not forever," she said, "but you need to clean the yeast out and get to know what your body needs. After that, you can eat more consciously."

I held my breath and nodded like, "Sure, I get it," even though I didn't. My muffin in the morning, my bagel for lunch, pasta with bread, and a couple glasses of wine with dinner and those were the things I did. They felt safe to me, they were what I understood, I didn't want to change.

Maria Elena watched me and she must have seen the door of my mind closing. She got up then and took out a bunch of flyers, all this information about cleansing, about yeast, about diet, and about the books I should read. She piled blue flyers, yellow flyers, and green flyers in front of me.

"Change is hard, Jennifer, it takes time and work," she said. "Just listen to your body and it will show you the way."

I shuffled her deck of flyers into one neat pile of rainbow colors and folded the whole thing in half.

"You call me if you have any questions," she said, "okay?"

I pushed all her flyers into my purse and stood to go.

"Sure," I said. "I will, Maria, I'll call you."

Maria Elena got up too, and I put my hand out between us to shake.

Maria Elena rolled her eyes and grabbed ahold of me then. She put her arms around my shoulders and gave me this bear of a hug which was probably all right; after all, the woman had seen my yeast. I patted her back with my one free hand. My purse was smashed between us.

"Well, thanks a lot, Maria Elena," I said, taking backward steps out of the room.

She kept ahold of my arm, her hand squeezing it while she smiled and nodded.

"Good luck, Jennifer," she said.

Two years later, I'm back at Dr. Green's office, only now it's with Josephine.

She's on the examining table, balanced with her hands against the wall.

"Ta ta ta," she says.

"Yeah," I say, "you're standing up, aren't you?"

She drops to her bottom, digs her hands into the white paper that covers the table and tears it to shreds.

There is a knock on the door and Dr. Green comes in, the same beard, the same glasses and a tie with monkeys riding motorcycles.

Josephine sets her eyes on him and opens them wide, the way she does with strangers.

"Who are you?" he says in a high voice like he's talking for Jo, and then he laughs at his own joke.

He shuts the door and puts a hand out for me to shake.

"Hi, Jennifer," he says. "Long time no see."

I put my hand in his and it's a quick shake, his hand cool in my own.

"It has been a while," I say.

"It has," he says, nodding. "We never see Spencer anymore."

I put a hand on Josephine's bare back and rub in a small circle.

"Nope," I say, "we've been great."

"That's what we like," Dr. Green says, "kids who stay healthy."

I laugh to be polite, but the truth is I've got one foot out of the whole modern medicine thing now. Since talking to Rebecca and seeing Maria Elena, I've changed everything about the way we eat. No more refined foods, no white sugar, no white flour, almost no soda or candy, and I get all our food at the organic grocery store. I have Spencer on special oils and vitamin C and the two of us are so healthy, we haven't had one infection for two years.

Still, I can't quite give Dr. Green up. He's like a dysfunctional boyfriend who still has some good points.

Dr. Green has Jo's file under his arm and he puts it on the counter and pulls his stool from under the examining table.

"So what have we got here?" he says.

"She's got a rash," I say.

Dr. Green opens a drawer, takes out a pair of latex gloves, and snaps them on his hands.

"Let's take a look," he says.

I lay Jo on the shredded white paper and he opens her diaper.

She's as still as a doll under my hand, but her head moves to look at Dr. Green, then back to look at me and back down to see him again.

"Everything is fine, baby," I say, "he's going to help."

Her pink rose petal self is a bloodred with angry skin peeling away to the next layer that's sticky and even more angry.

"This is a bad one," Dr. Green says, "tell me what you've done."

I stand up a little taller and talk with the authority of someone who wants to be good. A good daughter? A good mother? A good person?

"Okay," I say, "this came on as small red dots around Christmas. She was eating new things, cookies and citrus mostly, but I took her off that stuff right away."

Dr. Green shakes his head.

"It doesn't look like an allergy."

"We spent some time in a hot tub," I say, "and I've used vitamin E cream, which didn't really help, and then I called your nurse and she said it might be yeast so I tried a little yeast cream, but that didn't do anything either."

He moves his fingers around on her.

"Well," Dr. Green says, "it could be bacterial. Have you tried something like Neosporin?"

"I did think of that, but I wasn't sure if it was safe."

Dr. Green reaches long for a jar of giant Q-tips and unscrews the lid.

"Try it," he says, "in the meantime, I'll test her for an infection."

Jo wiggles to get up, but Dr. Green puts a hand on her stomach to keep her flat.

"She sure seems happy," he says, swabbing a sample from around her behind.

He lets her go and sticks the swab into a tube.

"Go ahead with the Neosporin," he says, "and someone from the office will call you in the morning with the test results."

I keep Jo on her back long enough to get her diaper back on and then I lift her to sit up.

"Do you think she'll need antibiotics?" I say.

Dr. Green writes something in Jo's chart and shrugs at the same time.

"Could be," he says, "but let's wait for the test."

I take Josephine under the arms, lift her off the table, and put her on my lap.

"I don't like antibiotics," I say, "I don't want to use them unless I absolutely have to."

I pull Jo's shirt over her head and tug her arms through the armholes.

Dr. Green closes Josephine's chart, stands up, and slides his stool under the table again.

"That's a good thing," he says, "I wish more parents were like you."

He puts Jo's file under his arm and watches me get her dressed, as if he knows I have more to say.

I don't say anything though. I pull a pink sock on Jo's foot and pull the other one on the other foot.

"Well, see you later, cutie," he says, putting a finger on Jo's nose and she still watches him like he's from another planet.

"Talk to you soon," I say.

"Yep," Dr. Green says, "one of the nurses will call."

He opens the door then and leaves without looking back, the door closing behind him with a click.


The next day, I'm on hold listening to doctor's office music mixed with the hiss of static. I can almost make out the sound of what was once an Elton John song.

A voice breaks the sound in half.

"This is the nurse," she says.

"I'm returning a message about Josephine," I say.

Through the telephone, I hear the shuffle of papers.

"Right," the nurse says, "she does have an infection and we've called in a prescription for antibiotics."

I'm in the car, on the way to an appointment, and I have my cell phone balanced on my shoulder while I make a right turn.

In the past twenty-four hours, Jo's bottom has gotten a little better on the Neosporin, but it's still bad. My gut says, hang on, wait, don't rush to the drugs, but then there's that old voice that says, you might be wrong.

"Well," I say. "Can I ask a question?"

"Okay," the nurse says.

"I've been reading a lot about antibiotics and one book recommends taking an antiyeast medication with them, you know, to prevent an overgrowth in her digestive tract."

"Oh, that's not necessary," the nurse says.

"Oh," I say. "Why?"

"We don't prescribe antiyeast medication unless the child actually has yeast," she says, "and the chance of that happening is one in five thousand."

I move with the flow of traffic.

"Wow, one in five thousand, really," I say. "Well, maybe you can ask Dr. Green for me anyway."

"Dr. Green is very busy today," the nurse says.

"I'm sure he is," I say, "but it will only take a second."

"I can already tell you," she says. "We don't prescribe antiyeast medicine with antibiotics."

"I'd like the doctor to call me and tell me this himself."

"Really," the nurse says, "it's not necessary, she won't need it."

I'm at the on-ramp for the freeway and I'm behind a car

with its brake lights on, the two of us waiting for the light to change.

I'm not sure why, but the woman on the telephone line makes me so angry, I just snap.

"Look," I say, "I am this child's mother and I know she will have a problem with yeast."

My voice in the car is this great, strong woman voice, only I'm shaking while I talk.

"I am not going to wait until she has a problem," I say, "I want to prevent a problem, so you why don't you tell Dr. Green what I want and have him call me."

The light changes and the car ahead of me pulls on the freeway ramp. I move too, both hands on the steering wheel while I hold the phone to my ear with my shoulder.

"Fine," the nurse finally says, "I'll have Dr. Green call you."

She hangs up on me and I snap my own phone closed.

"Fine, yourself," I say.

Two hours later, I pull into the parking lot of the grocery store, my last stop of the day, and my phone rings.

"Jennifer?" Dr. Green says. "What's going on?"

I stop the car and turn off the engine.

"Hi, Dr. Green," I say. "I was asking about an antiyeast medication for Jo to go with the antibiotics."

"Hmmm," Dr. Green says. "We don't usually do that since there is no study that shows a correlation between yeast over-growth and antibiotics."

"That may be, Dr. Green," I say, "but I've had a problem with yeast, Spencer has had a problem with yeast, and I really don't want to create a problem for Josephine."

I talk to him then, really talk about the doctors I've been

reading, this guy named Lendon Smith and this other doctor who wrote a book called *Super Immunity,* and how there are studies that do show a connection between yeast and antibiotics.

"She might not need any of it," I say, "so far the Neosporin is working, so I'd like to wait on the antibiotics anyway."

Dr. Green is quiet and then speaks in a tone I haven't heard before. Not mad, not disagreeing, more surprised and almost agreeable.

"If she's looking better, wait," he says, "and I guess an anti-yeast medication can't hurt her, so I'll call it in too. Is that good?"

"That's very good, Dr. Green," I say, "Thank you."

I press the off button on my cell phone and sit in the quiet of the car.

Out the window, people push shopping carts to and from the store and I see my own reflection in the windshield of the car, my narrow face and my glasses at a cockeyed angle.

All my life, I've looked at myself in the mirror and wondered, when will I grow up. When will I become a woman?

I thought it would happen when I started my period.

I thought it would happen when I got married.

I thought it would happen when I had a baby.

I've done all those things but so much of me has been frozen in the form of a little girl who looks out to people in positions of power and authority for the answers. Since power and authority are such male qualities, I guess I've just wanted to believe in men, I've wanted to believe so badly that I've doubted myself rather than question them.

Here I am, doing the same thing. I waited for Dr. Green to

call and say it was okay to have an antiyeast medication, I wanted him to say it was okay if I held off on using antibiotics, I even said "thank you," when he gave me these bits of approval, as if he did something for me. Dr. Green didn't do anything for me. I didn't need to thank him. I knew what I knew from my gut and my own experience and the knowledge should be enough. Maybe that is the growing up part.

I'm still in between being a child and a woman, I can see it right there in my reflection but I adjust my glasses to be straight and stop looking at myself for a while.

I've got groceries to buy and children to take care of.

PART THREE

# THE FUTURE

*Let yourself be silently drawn*
*by the stronger pull of what you really love.*

—RUMI

# THE ORCHID

It's a sunny afternoon in April and warm winds blow sweet spring off the jasmine vines that climb the pillars of the front porch.

Women come up the steps in pairs or one at a time and all of them have a book, either under their arm or tucked in their purses. In my grandma's day, a gathering of this size would have been the bridge club. In my mother's, it would have been the bowling league. Today, we call it the book group. No matter what you call it though, it's mostly a time for women to be together and to get away from house, husbands, and endless cries of "Mom."

Stephanie is the host and she opens the door to her guests and every time she does she says the same thing, "Come in, come in, we've been waiting for you."

In Stephanie's living room, I sit on the sofa next to a woman named Sue. Sue is heavy on her cushion and she wears a dress made of something soft, like rayon or silk, and the color of the fabric is between mango and peach.

"I hear you just had a baby," Sue says.

"Yes," I say, "she's two months old."

Sue pats at her heart, making the ruffle around her neck lift and fall like a gentle clap.

"Oh," Sue says, "a girl. You are so lucky. What's her name?"

Stephanie's at the door again, "Come in, come in, we've been waiting for you," and I hear myself talk about Josephine.

Stephanie looks fantastic over there with her hair styled in pretty curls around her face, her flawless makeup, and her trim body. She's the mother of three boys, she works, she volunteers at her church, she raises money for her kids' private schools, and she has been married to the same man forever. How is she doing it? How is she holding this gathering here, in her perfect house? What is the secret and how can I pry it out of her?

"Do you have pictures?" Sue says.

"Pictures?" I hear myself say. "Oh, sure, of course."

I pull out photos.

Stephanie shuts the door and glides into the dining room to move a platter of salmon in filo an inch closer to the bowl of strawberries. Her table looks good enough for van Gogh to paint.

Maybe, deep down, she has an eating disorder.

"And this is Spencer," I say. "He just loves his little sister. You know, I thought I would have a problem with him, but he's been just great."

A woman walks over to Stephanie and the two of them chat together. Stephanie laughs with her head back, completely relaxed.

Maybe she's on drugs.

"This is when Spencer was a baby himself," I say. "He was such a cutie. People say he looks like his sister, but I don't see it."

Stephanie claps her hands over the sound of women's voices.

"Please eat," she says, "there's plenty of food and tea, just help yourselves."

Maybe Stephanie is just a perfect woman.

Sue is buried in photos of Josephine and Spencer and I don't remember the last time she spoke.

"Here's another one of Spencer holding the baby," I say. "He's so gentle with her."

Sue takes the photo by its edge, but she's not with me anymore. She's wise to my distraction and has set her own attention to the table and the food.

"Isn't that sweet," she says.

I follow Sue's lead and spot a three-layer chocolate cake that makes my mouth water. Given free rein, I'd eat the whole thing right now, that's how much I hate myself compared to Stephanie.

I make myself stop talking about the kids and gather up their photos.

Sue makes her escape and I sort through the photos but don't see the details of them anymore. What the hell is the matter with me? How did I become a person who is about as interesting as a brick of cheese? I push the pictures back into my wallet. Who am I anyway?

The spring of 1988 was the last time I really knew who I was. In the spring of 1988, I was divorced and happy about it, I was a television reporter, I had a sweet little dog for company, and I had my own place that was beautiful and quiet and safe.

In the spring of 1988, I was dating Steve.

"This is nothing like your place," Steve said. "Don't be shocked."

Steve was holding the screen door open with his shoulder and working his key on the deadbolt while I stood at the bottom of the stoop with my arms crossed tight. My face was arranged neutral, like Switzerland.

I was already passing judgment though, and Steve was right. There were cobwebs over the mailbox, dead bugs in the light fixture over the front door, and from the looks of things, the key didn't even work in his rusty lock.

Steve worked the lock with hard twists of his wrist and the deadbolt finally tumbled.

"There we go," Steve said.

He pushed at the door and old air rushed at us.

"Anyone here?" he called into the hall.

Quiet came back and Steve shined his smile my way.

He was a heart stopper. He was tall and wide-shouldered and had wild dark hair that fell over his forehead, forcing him to push it back like an afterthought. All that would have been enough, but Steve's secret weapon was his smile. When he turned it on full blast the way he did, it made his blue eyes shimmer gold. Since the day I met him, almost a month earlier, it was his smile that had tumbled the deadbolt of my heart.

"Looks like we've got the place to ourselves," he said. "Come on in."

He offered a hand and I took it.

We went into the shadows of the hall and inside, it was

cold and the windows were blocked from the outside by over-grown bushes. The only natural light was what squeaked through thick leaves and branches.

We stopped where the hall split to kitchen, living room, and a couple of closed doors to other rooms.

"So this is home," I said.

Steve let go of my hand and pushed into the front pockets of his jeans.

"It's a place to crash," he said, "your place is more like home."

I did this wide-eyed nod thing.

In the kitchen, the counters were crowded with dirty dishes and open boxes of cereal, the stove had a couple of dirty pans on cold burners, and the sink was loaded with more dishes. The smell was sour milk and old garbage.

Steve rushed into the kitchen, turned on water at the sink, and picked up two bowls from the counter.

"Sorry it's such a mess," he said.

He took up a washcloth and flopped it around in a bowl, but I left him and went to the living room. Steve turned the water off and followed me.

"I never leave the kitchen like that," he said.

He picked up dirty socks, inside-out jeans, and wadded T-shirts.

"And this is all my roommate's stuff," he said.

I stepped over newspapers spread on the floor.

"I'm going to have to talk to him about this place," Steve said, "what a mess."

I nodded reassurance that said, "I know, honey, I know," and pointed to a closed door.

"What's in there?" I said.

Steve tossed the wad of clothes in a pile by the TV.

"That's my room," he said, "go ahead. Go on in."

On the other side of the door, his room was a twin mattress on the floor, a tangle of sheets in the middle of the bed, and more dirty clothes and newspapers. I let the door open all the way and it banged up against the wall.

"You're right, Steve," I said, "you're a total neat freak."

Steve laughed and went in ahead of me.

"Sorry," he said.

He pulled his sheets straight on the bed, which wasn't big enough for a teenager.

"I figure, what's the use in making it when you're getting back in a few hours later, right?"

The way he made his bed showed it wasn't a habit. Even when he got it straightened up, it was still a mess.

I shouldered up to the doorjamb and within a few minutes of being there, he had changed from the person a month of dating had built in my mind. I knew he was one of those late bloomers, a twenty-seven-year-old college student who sold life insurance on the side, but I guess I hoped for more. I hoped, at the very least, he knew how to pick up after himself. I would have been happy if he just had furniture, but he had almost nothing. The dark space was appointed with milk crates turned over to make shelves and the few pieces of his clothes were folded on top in separate piles for pants, T-shirts, and boxer shorts. Next to his bed was another overturned milk crate that held a lamp, a clock, and a photograph in a small plastic frame.

I went the rest of the way into his room and the picture was a man and a woman leaned on a wooden slat fence. They stood with a wide space between them, close to three feet, and in proportion to the size of the fence, they seemed pretty small.

Steve snapped the lamp on.

"My folks," he said.

"Really?" I said.

"Yep," he said.

I looked again, but they didn't look anything like Steve.

"They look nice," I said.

Steve nodded.

Past his folks, there was a white page of paper taped to the wall and the writing was a thin careful print.

"What's this?" I said.

"Just this thing I did in a class," he said.

The page was part in the lamplight and part in the shadows. I moved the lamp over so it was all in the light.

It was a grid with the years from 1988 to the year 2000 written along the bottom line. Above 1989, it read, "Graduate from college," and then, in 1990 there was an arrow that pointed to "Perfect job with benefits." Farther down in 1991, it read, "Buy Porsche with cash," 1993 read, "Get married," 1996, "Have kids." Directly after those words, he had a question mark.

"Don't you want kids?" I said.

He took one shoulder up in a shrug, like a man playing poker who didn't want to show his cards.

"Depends if I find the right girl," he said, nodding my way. "How about you?"

I leveled a look right back at him, after all, I was born in Nevada. I knew plenty about the bluff.

"I might need to find the right girl too," I said.

Steve was quiet and then he laughed out loud.

I laughed too, but I was pretty sure he didn't catch my meaning, and I was also sure he didn't realize that one of the really big questions was between us now. It wasn't this neutral "Do you like kids?" it was "Do you want kids?" with the underlying "Do you want kids with me?"

Up until now, we had been kissing for hours, eating ice cream and strawberries at midnight and having five-hour telephone conversations.

Up until now, I was amped into a super version of me, this funny, sexy, pulled-together chick with a retro vintage place, a whole repertoire of snappy recipes, and a fancy television news career that made me unique.

Up until now, it was fun, but I could see we were on the way to the place where someone was going to say, "I love you."

Love, the great equalizer that leads us down possession's path.

I had been down that path before, married four years and a nasty divorce because I wasn't ready for kids. That man had since remarried and was up to three boys.

Since my divorce, I had sworn there would be no more spins on the ride of love since it was always a ride that stopped at the question of marriage and kids, but now I was standing in a man's bedroom looking at his lifeline and considering the question: Did I want kids?

It wasn't just one question. To my mind, it was a thousand questions.

When did I want kids?

How many kids did I want?

What kind of mother would I be?

What kind of mother did he expect me to be?

What kind of father would he be?

What kind of father would I expect him to be?

Who would take care of the kids, when we had them?

Who would make the money?

How could I possibly imagine these answers when I was so far ahead on my own timeline? Without writing a thing down, I put myself through college, had four years into the perfect career with benefits, and had my own plans to climb up the ladder of journalism. Steve would need a long time to catch up, if he caught up, and when that happened who knew where I'd be.

My practical mind doused the fires of our new love and left the charred smell of reality behind.

I moved my finger to the end of his lifeline.

"What happens in 2000?" I said.

Steve's face lifted in one of his great smiles and he stepped my way to close the distance between us.

"It's just the end of this plan," he said.

He pressed his hands at the curve of my waist, and made his smile all bold.

"When we get to the year 2000," he said, "I'll do another."

He pressed his hips against the flat of my pelvis and the fires weren't out after all.

"We," as in, we were going to be a couple.

He moved in closer, licking his lips to make them wet.

"We," as in, he'd be seeing me in the year 2000.

I pressed my hands to his chest.

"We," as in, you and me?

I leaned back to see into his blue eyes. I was still trying to be a me. I wasn't sure if I was ready to be a "we," but there he was, with that smile.

"I suppose I could help you find a job," I said. "I know all about writing résumés and pestering people to get interviews. I could help you with that part."

"That would be great," he said.

Steve pressed his hand into the small of my back and moved the other one behind my neck.

"And you could teach me a few things about saving money," I said. "I am the worst."

Steve nodded his lips against mine and closed his eyes.

I kept my eyes open though, I guess I didn't need all the answers to all the questions, after all, life was a great mystery. Besides Steve wasn't just a fresh young man who didn't know how to pick up after himself. He was still all the other things he was before and more. He was way ahead of other guys. He had a lifeline. He had a plan.

Steve moved his arms all the way around my body and brought me in closer, if that was possible, and I got lost in the feel of him and that wild chemistry that we shared. I moved my arms around his neck and, finally, I closed my eyes.

Seven years later, my eyes were wide open under the light of the chandelier hanging in our dining room. It was one of those sparkling wonders Steve saved when we renovated our house and even though it had a dimmer switch for kinder light, Steve had the thing cranked to the highest setting.

It was six in the morning, a time that begged for shadows, but there he was under the thousand-wattage bulbs, messing with his suitcase.

I sat in one of the heavy wood chairs at the end of the table, eyes squinted to dim the light in my own head.

The only sound was Steve zipping and unzipping bags, but in the air between us, were things unspoken. Things like how he wouldn't sleep with me last night and how he said, "I need a good night of rest; after all, I have to work." There was also how his work took him away from the house, days at a time, leaving me here to run the whole domestic show. There was how he had the nerve to complain about his job too, a job that gave him freedom, money, and long, liquid nights of unbroken sleep.

I jumped at the sound of his voice.

"What?" I said.

"My dry cleaning," he said, "would you mind dropping it off for me?"

I moved my robe to cover my legs under the table.

"Sure, I'll drop it for you."

"And you should call someone about the drain in the basement," he said.

"Right," I said, "I'll do that too."

My voice sounded as bright as the light over us. I hated the way I sounded.

"So you'll be back when?" I said.

Steve put his microphone into his briefcase and took out his calendar book. He flipped it open and turned the pages, moving his finger over the dates.

"Thursday," he said, "and I have that auction in California this weekend, remember?"

I twisted all of my hair into a ponytail, tighter and tighter against the nape of my neck.

"Oh yeah," I said, "of course, great, no really, that's great."

Steve put the calendar book back into his briefcase.

"I told you I was going," he said.

"Yeah," I said, "I know you did. I know."

Steve zipped his suitcase closed and he was in that final place where he'd say good-bye, kiss me quick, and disappear.

"Well, I hate to leave you guys," Steve said.

"Well, we hate to see you go," I said, my voice light and bright.

I pushed the chair back from the table, except it was so heavy it caught on the rug and the wood scraped at the back of my knees.

"Darn it," I said.

I lifted the chair by the arms and forced it back, getting myself up to say a proper good wife good-bye. I smoothed my robe again and readjusted the tie around my waist.

Steve put his briefcase over his shoulder, picked up his suitcase, and gave me this one-eye look, the other eye shut like he was trying to see through a telescope.

"Are you going to be all right?" he said.

I scooted the chair under the table, but it caught on the rug again.

"All right?" I said.

I lifted it up and shoved it so hard, it banged against the table and made the whole thing shake.

"Why wouldn't we be all right?" I said.

The sound of my voice gave me away, the tone dropping to match mood.

Steve's eyes went wide and he spoke very carefully.

"I didn't say you wouldn't be all right," he said.

I crossed my arms one way and then the other.

"What are you saying?" I said. "Don't you think I can handle it here or something?"

His eyes went even wider.

"I just know you're tired, Jen," he said. "I worry about you here all alone."

I decided it was better to have my arms crossed right over left so I stayed that way and leveled a hard look at him.

"You know what, you're right. I *am* tired. I'm exhausted. But that doesn't seem to matter since I don't have a real job like you and I don't need a real night of sleep."

Steve was pressed and dressed for work, his hair combed back and still damp from his shower, and his face shaved clean. All cleaned and still like he was, he looked like a mannequin in a store.

I filled the quiet he made with a storm of how I was here doing all the things for the house that took every extra second of my time and juggling Spencer at the same time and how I did it on no sleep and a ton of disrespect and that he had another think coming if he thought I was on some glorious vacation.

He put his suitcase on the table and pushed at his hair.

"I'll drop my own dry cleaning when I get back," he said. "Jeez."

"This isn't about dry cleaning, Steve," I said. "This is about you working and acting like your work is so important and me not working and the idea that what I do around here doesn't even deserve the luxury of sleep."

Steve twisted his face from his nose out, like a sneeze coming on, and he had no idea what I just said.

I spread my arms wide to the room, the house, the baby, the world of being a housewife.

"I can't do this," I said, "I have to have my own job, I have to make my own money, I have to do something more than this."

Steve leaned to the table, balancing himself on his fists.

"Well, get a job then," he said.

I leaned on the table too, my face into his face.

"I thought one of us was supposed to stay home," I said, "I thought that's what we agreed, I thought day care was too expensive."

Steve stood off the table, flipping a hand at all our plans.

"Forget that," he said, "just get a job. Anything would be better than listening to you complain."

I stood up too and threw my arms wide.

"Oh," I said, "you can complain about your job, but I can't complain that I don't have a job?"

Steve opened his mouth and closed it again.

I leaned into the big built-in piece of furniture that held all the china we inherited from Steve's grandmother, and put my hand over my eyes.

"Look," I said, "I'm sorry to argue, but I'm lost right now. I have no idea what I want to do and I'm not sure how to balance Spencer with some kind of job."

My voice was all the way in my stomach, vibrating down to my feet.

"I know we talked about one of us being home with the kids and since I'm not working, that person is me and I want

to be here with Spencer, I do," I say, "but I need to do something. I need to make my own money. I need to work. I could
do some freelance promotions, I could write, I could do a lot
of things. I just don't know what to do."

Steve stood across from me, but he wasn't with me anymore. There was this flat shift in his eyes, like he had his
mind made up.

"You know," he said, "I remember when we met and you
had your career in TV news. You thought you were so hot and
now, you are in the same place I was. You have no idea what
you want to do or be. It's interesting, isn't it?"

From my feet to my neck, my whole body was stiff.

"What's interesting about it?" I said.

"That the shoe is on the other foot," he said. "Now you
know how I used to feel."

Steve looked at his watch, time to go and quick, before I
recovered, leaned over to kiss me. His lips barely touched my
forehead.

He was gone ten minutes, maybe more, before I could hear
anything around me, before I could even think.

Outside, the dawn broke up the dark and in the window,
the chandelier reflected its high beams on the glass.

I measured myself against each breath and went to the
light switch, dimming it at last.

I pulled a chair out from the table again and sat down.

The hardest thing to hear is the truth.

I moved my hands over the top of the table and the wood
was smooth under my hands.

Steve was right. Before we got married, he didn't even
know what he wanted to do and I worked at a job I adored. I

don't know if I thought I was hot stuff, but I was confident, I was focused and I knew what I wanted, I even tried to help Steve find his way but my help made him defensive, as if he wasn't a man if he didn't do it on his own. Still, our amazing chemistry kept us coming back for more of each other and we got married. After the wedding, Steve's career took off. Together we bought an old house, fixed it up, and I was so distracted taking care of the house and then taking care of Spencer, that I let my work go. I did some freelance work from the house, but soon I let that go too. Now I was here, a mother, a wife, and a person full of doubt. How could I have let myself go? How was I going to get myself back?

If things stayed like they were right now, my title would be "housewife," otherwise known as "the little woman." There would be years of greeting cards that came my way on Mother's Day and they'd be filled with sentiments that said a mother is more precious than a fresh morning dew. I'd get a few clay handprints, piles of kid art, and then, the rest of every year, Steve and Spencer and maybe another kid would go on to their dreams. In twenty years, I would have raised my children and taken good care of my husband and the house, but that would be about it. They would all have their lives and they would have been my life.

I loved my home, I loved Steve, and I adored Spencer, but I couldn't be just a mother and a wife. I would end up bitter and angry and I'd blame Steve when the truth was, I'd have no one to blame but myself.

I turned my hands up and in my empty palm were all the lines, the lifeline, the heartline, the lines to the past, to the present and to the future. I wished I could read all those lines and know what would come next. I wished I knew what to do but in the void of not knowing, I had to talk. Maybe I had to fight.

I got up and went to the telephone, punched in the cellular number in Steve's car, and pressed the telephone to my ear.

Over the next three years, the fight for more from my life was with Steve. He argued about the high cost of childcare, complained said childcare wasn't good enough for Spencer and when it came his turn to take care of a fussy Spencer, even made bitter comments about how "good mothers stay home." Steve complained I wasn't doing what he thought I should be doing, he said my work wasn't that interesting (to him) and he didn't understand why I would want to become a writer who wrote books about her own life.

"It's so personal," he said, "everyone will know everything about you."

Every step of the way, I stayed on my course and fought back for a future beyond stay-at-home mother and adoring wife. I wrote out of the house during Spencer's naps, I wrote at the library when Steve was home, I wrote when a baby-sitter came over and took Spencer to the park. Eventually, when all that writing paid off, Steve didn't have any more complaints. Once I was paying my way, he was a fast convert to the benefits of the working woman.

My next move was to rent an office, make a schedule, and call myself a professional.

Then I got pregnant with Josephine.

Just when I had life figured out, another baby came and I was home again. Someone had to breast-feed, someone had to stay close to the house and the baby, someone had to cushion

Spencer's bumpy transition from only child to older brother and of course, that someone was me. Domestication, even temporary, brought the battle back, only this time, I wasn't fighting with Steve. This time, and likely before, I was fighting with myself, or an ideal of myself. Was I going to be a person who put her kids and home first, "the good mother," or was I going to be a person who put herself first, "the selfish bitch"?

It was a battle of extremes, yes, but I was there, fighting both ends of the spectrum.

Stephanie claps her hands over the top of her head.

"Ladies, ladies," she says, "it's just about time to get started."

Women take last bites, wipe mouths with napkins, and brush crumbs off dresses and pants.

Stephanie puts a manicured hand on my shoulder.

"Before we start," she says, "I've got something for you."

She does this little hook of the head and I get up, smooth my hands over my skirt, and follow her to the kitchen.

In here the refrigerator is littered with kid art, telephone numbers, and clippings from newspapers and magazines. A pair of muddy shoes sits on the mat by the back door, there is dog hair all over her kitchen rug, and the sliding glass door leading to the backyard is covered with dog slobber and handprints.

Here is the evidence I was looking for. Turns out Stephanie is human after all.

Stephanie does an elegant hand wave at a small potted orchid with four white tissue blooms of real perfection. The center of each flower is a burst of purple and its long stem is trained elegant up a stick.

"I wanted to give you this," she says, "as a kind of thanks for your beautiful book and for just being you."

There is a strange quiet between us, this odd beat of nothing that I should jump into with gratitude but I don't. I don't even see this as a gift. It's one more task. It's number 101 on the list: become expert on exotic plants in time to keep orchid alive.

Great.

The fine lines of Stephanie's eyebrows lift, question marks over pretty green eyes.

I smile in what I hope translates into delight.

"Oh my goodness, Stephanie," I say, "thank you so much."

Stephanie's eyebrows go back to normal and she holds her hands over her heart. She goes on then, says how much she loved my book, how she identified with me, how brave and strong she thought I was, and in all her talk, I'm caught behind the veil of opposing worlds. There is her perception of me (much higher than I have) and my perception of me (much lower than is accurate) and there is the reality of this inner fight within the question: What am I going to do now?

Do I give up writing?

Do I stay home and be the mother?

Can I write and be home?

Is it right to do both?

Am I a bad person for wanting it all?

Is it possible to have it all?

The fight of questions is strong but outside, in the world of Stephanie's kitchen, I'm in the polite stance of gratitude and humility. I nod to what Stephanie is saying but pay almost no attention.

Wouldn't it be nice to drop the polite act and talk straight, one woman trying to be perfect to another? Couldn't I just say, "Look lady, don't give me a goddamned orchid right now. You've got it all figured out, obviously, but I don't. I have a new baby, a son, a house that's a mess, not to mention that I'm supposed to volunteer my obligatory twenty-five hours at my kid's kindergarten class, drop thirty pounds, pay the bills, and get some groceries in the refrigerator before my kids starve. I can't keep this slice of floral perfection alive. I can barely keep my kids and myself alive. What in the world are you trying to do to me here, break my back under the weight of yet another demand to keep life going? How much more life can I be responsible for anyway? Huh? Huh?"

Poor Stephanie. What would she do with that little slice of reality?

She'd say, "It's a gift. I just wanted to give you a gift and you have now shattered my illusion. You are a selfish bitch."

Thank God, a woman enters the scene in search of the bathroom.

"Of course," Stephanie says.

As she leaves, Stephanie touches a finger to my arm, smiling.

"I'll see you out in the living room," she says.

I swallow reality and keep my own smile in place.

"Yes," I say. "I'll be right there."

Stephanie leads the other woman away and the swinging door of the kitchen closes me in with my thoughts.

I rub at the space between my eyes.

The orchid sits there, silent, perfect, a challenge, a test, an enemy.

I turn the pot on the counter and the white and purple flowers bounce a little on the ends of their delicate stems.

The women talk in the living room and I can feel everyone waiting for me to get in there.

I touch the petal of one of the flowers and the texture is soft but thick. It's a lot sturdier than it looks. I press down a little harder, almost enough to pull the flower off but when I let go, it bounces up and down in this impossible balance between stability and instability.

Sometimes a gift is just a gift but sometimes, when you are desperate for meaning amid confusion, a gift can be a metaphor.

My questions have been about right and wrong but maybe this is about balance. I have another child now and I'm off balance, okay. When it was just Steve, Spencer, and me, it was hard work but we achieved balance. Now it's time to see if we can do it again. If I must work, then I must work. If I want more, then I will have more. If I want to achieve perfection, good luck. Perfection is a flower in a pot. I'm flawed in the form of a human. In the end, we're both going to die.

The flower doesn't agree or disagree. It's just there, still and quiet, beautiful and elegant.

"Fine," I say. "I guess you're coming home with me."

## THE FIRST PANCAKE

Spencer and I are in the kitchen making pancakes. I pour the batter into the pan and Spencer stands by with a spatula.

"Wait for it to get all bubbly," I say, "then turn it."

He stands on a step stool he's pushed next to the stove and I've tied a dish towel around his waist.

Josephine sleeps late this morning and I have the baby monitor plugged in by the coffeepot.

"Can I put chocolate chips on it?" Spencer says.

"You don't want to waste them," I say, "the first one is usually no good, remember?"

"Sometimes the first one is good," he says.

"That's true," I say. "Go ahead then."

Spencer drops four chocolate chips into the pancake and it bubbles in the pan. It makes me nervous to have him so close to the heat, but I keep my distance, letting him do the work.

He slides the spatula under and turns the pancake, but it folds over on itself.

"Ew," he says, "it's ruined."

"That's okay," I say, "we'll try it again."

Three pancakes and a couple sausages later, Spencer wipes syrup off his face with a paper towel.

"I'm full," he says.

Josephine makes her little dove call through the monitor and Spencer's eyes get big.

"Is that Jo?" he says.

I put his dirty dishes into the sink.

"Sounds like it," I say.

He jumps off his stool.

"Can I go up?" he says.

"Sure," I say.

Spencer runs out of the kitchen and up the steps like it's Christmas morning.

I wipe the counter down and throw the dishrag into the sink. Through the monitor, Spencer's in her room and talking in his high, happy voice.

"Hi Jo, Jo baby," he says.

She talks back in her own "ta ta ta" chatter and by the time I get to the nursery, he's pushed a stool over and lowered the side of her crib. He leans into the bed, half cradling and half flopping her in a sitting position.

"Hold her extra careful, Spencer," I say. "She can't sit up like that yet."

Spencer keeps his hand at her neck as he eases her back.

"I know," Spencer says. "She's a delicate flower."

"That's right," I say.

I lean on one end of her crib and Josephine moves her eyes off Spencer and looks at me. Her arms and legs kick with a double dose of happiness. First Spencer and now Mom, can it get any better than this?

I put a hand on her tummy and roll her side to side.

"Morning, Jo Jo," I say.

She kicks her feet and whacks at the air. Spencer laughs out loud.

"She's so happy all the time," he says.

"It true," I say. "She's a happy baby."

At the same age, Spencer wasn't happy at all. He was fussy and cranky and never slept through the night until he was more than eight months old. Maybe it was just his temperament, maybe it was the curse of being the firstborn, or maybe it was the fact that I was such an amateur that he could smell the worry that lifted out of my pores.

"Can I change her diaper?" Spencer says.

"Sure," I say.

I get the wipes and a fresh diaper from her dresser and Spencer goes to work on her outfit. He opens each snap with a little tug and she's all wiggle under his hands.

He pulls the tabs of Velcro of the diaper, takes ahold of the top of her diaper, and stops.

"If it's a poop, you have to do it."

"If it's a poop," I say, "I'll do it."

Spencer pulls the diaper down fast and cranes his chin to see.

"Just pee," he says.

"Okay," I say, "gentle now."

He lifts her legs and pulls the old diaper out.

"Good work," I say.

As if he's the surgeon and I'm the nurse in charge of the instruments, he hands me the dirty diaper and takes the clean one from my hand.

He lifts her legs again, snuggles the diaper under her butt and this is my cue to step in. I wipe her bottom and hold the new diaper over her tummy. Spencer grabs the tabs, pulls one side tight, and then pulls the other into place.

All the experts say a new baby is hard on the firstborn, but Spencer's doing just great.

He smoothes the tabs flat and puts her legs back into her outfit, one at a time. He moves out of the way.

"You can snap her back up," he says.

"Nice work," I say.

Spencer puts his hands on his hips.

"I'm good at this," he says.

"You are good at this."

"I am a good big brother," he says.

I put my hand on his shoulder and it's just a little knob of bone under my hand.

"You are a very good big brother."


That was April and then it becomes May, the month Spencer goes from four to five. According to a book called *Your Five-Year-Old*, Spencer's fifth year is expected to be both sunny and serene.

"You're stupid, Mom," Spencer says. "Mom's a big stupid poop head."

I back our car into a parking spot except I miss my mark and the back tire goes over the curb. I turn the steering wheel hard, angle the tires to the street again, and eyeball Spencer in the rearview mirror.

My voice is winter wind.

"What did I say about calling me names?"

"Don't say 'stupid,' don't say 'poop.'"

I check the side mirror and the traffic is clear. I pull out and line myself up for another shot at the parallel park.

"Stupid," Spencer says.

I turn the steering wheel left, then right, then left again, and I turn off the car.

"Sorry," Spencer says.

The kid makes me crazy and I think he must know it. First it's "poop head" and "stupid" and then he'll say "I'm sorry" until I say something.

I take my keys out of the ignition and turn in my seat to look at him face to face.

Jo's in her seat next to him, but she's turned the other way, cooing and kicking around.

I take a deep breath and make my voice as calm and patient as I can.

"We have to get your birthday stuff," I say. "We need invitations, we need all the party favors and bags for your friends. If you don't stop calling me names, we're going home and we'll forget the whole birthday thing."

Spencer listens, but I must be saying too many words because pretty soon, he's looking out the window, bored expression in his eyes.

"I need you to work with me," I say.

Spencer rolls his eyes my way.

"I know, I know," he says, "work with you, not against you."

I move my hand through the seats and put it on his knee.

"That's right," I say, "we've got Jo here, we've got things to do, let's just try to get along and when we get home, you can be as freaky as you want to be."

I squeeze into his knee.

"Can we do it?"

He nods one time, a solid up-and-down nod.

"Yes," he says, "we can do it."

"Good," I say.


Ten minutes later, we're curbside. Spencer's hand is in my right hand and Jo is nested in my left arm. Over my shoulder, I have the diaper bag with extra diapers, wipes, rattles, pacifiers, tissues, and an outfit, since you can never have too much stuff when you're out with a burping, spitting-up, pooping baby. They are active volcanoes that can blow at any time.

The street is four lanes and the cars move so fast, they make the air move fast too.

Spencer tugs to get free of my hand.

"I want to push the button," he says.

"You can push the button, but don't let go of me," I say.

He leans long and his hand is almost out of mine.

"You're making me nervous, Spence," I say, "stay back with me."

Spencer presses the button and steps back from the curb.

"You're always nervous," he says.

"You bet I am," I say, "one of those cars would squish you like a pancake. It's my job to keep you safe."

It's quiet for a second and I hear Spencer saying something to himself.

"Poop head," he whispers in a singsong of a voice. "Mom's a stupid poop head."

I shake his hand in my hand.

"Would you just stop it with that poop head stuff."

"Sorry," he says.

The light changes and the sign across the street reads WALK.

"Okay," I say, "let's go."

We get about halfway across and Spencer stops cold.

"What are you doing?" I say.

"My foot hurts," he says.

I shift Jo in my arm and Spencer's feet are in a pair of white tennis shoes. One of his laces is untied, but other than that, he's fine.

"You can't stop here," I say, "we have to cross."

Spencer takes one step, but it's this drag thing where his foot turns sideways and he pulls it behind him.

"I can't," he says.

He drops to his knees.

I tug on his arm.

"Spencer," I say, "get up."

"Ahhhh," he says, "I can't."

Past the lines of the crosswalk, cars stack up in the lanes and the sign on the other side of the street blinks with the DON'T WALK red hand.

I adjust the baby bag over my shoulder, hold the baby extra tight, and snake my arm around Spencer's back. I half carry, half drag him to the side of the street. The light changes and the traffic starts to flow.

When I let him go, he stands there, on both feet.

"Jesus, Spencer," I say. "What happened to you?"

"I don't know," he says.

"What do you mean, you don't know?" I say. "You don't just stop walking when we cross the street. That is so dangerous."

"My foot hurt," he yells, his hands open, palms up.

His lip starts that quiver thing that gets me every time.

With Jo snug against my side, I kneel down and touch around his ankle and foot. Jo's bag tilts on the sidewalk and a rattle rolls away, the pacifier case breaks open, and a couple diapers fall out.

"Was it a cramp?"

"No."

"Is something in your shoe?"

"No."

I roll back on my heels to look into his face.

It would be so much easier if he had one of those scrolling marquees on his head that said "I'm manipulating you right now because I need the attention," or "I just felt like having a little fun, but it didn't work out the way I thought," or "I had a twinge of pain, but it's gone now."

Josephine picks this time to cry and the sound of her is such a surprise, I jump a little. I get Jo tight to my chest and hold Spencer's hand.

"So your foot doesn't hurt now?" I say.

"No."

"And you think you can walk without falling down?"

"Yes."

"Are you sure, Spencer?" I say.

"Yes," he says.

Jo burps and nasty baby garp runs down the side of my neck.

I fish a blanket out of her bag, wipe Jo's face and my own neck.

"All right now," I say, shoving the blanket back into the bag, "this is fun, we are supposed to be having fun."

I pack her baby stuff back into her bag, push myself to stand, and take Spencer by the hand.

"Let's try this again," I say.

That night, candles burn, jazz plays on the stereo, and we sit in the dining room.

Spencer's at the head of the table, his Spiderman plate on a placemat of the world and he has chicken strips, French fries, and carrot sticks.

Jo's in the middle of the dining table in her bouncy vibrating chair and she's being hummed into an altered state of infant bliss.

I sit across from Steve and he's over there cutting his chicken with his knife. I lift my chin to Spencer while I cut my own chicken.

"Tell Dad what you're doing for your birthday party," I say.

Spencer dips his chicken strip into a puddle of barbeque sauce.

"Bowling," Spencer says.

"Bowling?" Steve says. "Really?"

"I called the bowling alley," I say, "and reserved two lanes."

"Yeah," Spencer says, "Joel is coming, and Eli and Pau too."

Spencer is full of the news about the invitations and how we're making these party bags for everyone.

"Mom bought all the stuff today," Spencer says and then he frowns, "but she won't let me have a balloon."

I stop cutting my chicken.

"I did let you have a balloon," I say. "Tell the truth."

"I want another one," he says, "I want a red one."

"Look," I say, talking to my food, "those are for the party, I let you have three balloons and that's enough, we're going to save the rest."

Steve still wears his work clothes, slacks and a button-down shirt, and he has this odd look on his face, like he has no idea what's going on and wants me to fill him in.

I shake my head at him with the answer, which is, "Don't ask."

Spencer crosses his arms over his chest and tucks in his chin.

"I don't care if you are mad at me or not," I say. "I gave you three. Three balloons are enough."

I cut my chicken into a dozen pieces, not even knowing that I'm doing it and I'm worn out from "poop," "stupid," the scare in the crosswalk, an argument in the paper store that ended with Spencer in tears and two hours of arguing about balloons. If spanking were in, I'd have him over my knee and paddle his butt good, but hitting him would just make everything worse. I'd still be mad, and on top of it, I'd be a child beater.

The quiet at the table simmers and Steve lifts above it to chat about work. I jump in to say that Jo is cutting a tooth.

Spencer has his face against his hand, elbow on the table as he chews. Then he starts to cough.

Steve reaches long and pats Spencer between his shoulders.

"Are you okay?" Steve says.

Spencer shakes his head that no, he's not okay, and his face goes red.

"He's choking," I say.

Steve gets up fast and pats Spencer with a little more force.

Spencer leans over his plate, opens his mouth, and a wad of chewed chicken falls out.

His dark eyes are round and huge the way they get when he's scared and he takes one of those deep inhales.

"Ahhhhh," he howls, "I can't eat, I can't eat."

"Whoa," Steve says. "You just had too much in your mouth, just try smaller bites."

I get up too and grab the tissue box. Steve takes two tissues for Spencer and wipes at his tears.

"You're okay, buddy," Steve says, "take it easy."

Josephine is the blank screen for the drama of us and after taking the whole scene in, she lets it back out with this loud howl that drags both of us away from Spencer.

"I got her," Steve says, "you eat, Jen."

"No," I say, "you've got Spencer, I'll get her."

I go to Josephine and scoop her up.

Steve calms Spencer and gets him set up with another plate of food.

I hold Jo against my heart, rocking side to side, and say this secret prayer of thanks. Even when she's hard, she's so easy compared to Spencer. I hate that I feel this way too. I wish I could just get back into the groove with him, but something is out of whack.

Steve sits down again and starts up with his dinner again.

"Go ahead and sit, Jen," Steve says. "Spencer's okay."

"I'm not hungry anymore," I say.

I leave my dinner on the table then and walk out of the dining room with Jo in my arms and Spencer on my mind.

\*          \*          \*

A week later, I'm on the floor and Spencer is still on my mind.

My arms and legs are wide in the pose of a dead body you'd see in an old gangster movie. The only thing I need now is the chalk outline.

The rug is itchy through my shirt, but I don't scratch at myself. Instead, I stare at the waves of too-thick plaster that someone put on the ceiling.

It's Spencer's birthday and this should be a good day, but this morning he threw a fit, stomped around, and called me names. I tried to ignore him, tried to be the happy mother who says, "Now, Spencer, we don't talk that way," but after about an hour of him I was just pissed off. When I took him and his little cupcakes to school, I couldn't get rid of him fast enough.

"Have a great day," I said.

"Yeah, yeah," Spencer said, going into his classroom without giving me a good-bye kiss.

Lying on the floor, I replay the whole thing in my head. It's rewind, pause, play, and my conclusion is simple. I've ruined him completely. I'm a terrible mother. I was terrible from the first day and after five years of trying to get it right, I've made nothing but mistakes. He's the first pancake, the one that always gets burned or folds in half.

There's a knock on the door and I roll my head back to see the world upside down.

Slavka's smiling face is in one of the squares of glass in the front door and she fogs the window with her breath.

I push myself off the floor.

Slavka is a blonde bubble of happiness with an Eastern European accent.

"Oh my God," she says, "it's Spencer's happy birthday today."

I make myself smile and push my hand through my hair.

"Yep," I say, "five years old."

She puts both her hands over her heart.

"Oh-my-God," she says, "he's such a big boy now, I remember him, just six months old, a little tiny baby and now, he's so big."

I close the door and she puts down her purse and shrugs off her coat, talking in her broken English the whole time.

Slavka came into my world when I first started to write out of the house, back when Spencer was six months old. She was with me, a few hours every week, until he was three. Now that Jo is here, she is back and I turn to her mostly so I can run errands and catch up on my sleep. I want to use her if I go back to writing, but deep down, I still can't decide when to go back to my work.

I walk from the living room to the kitchen, where I have my coat and my purse and Slavka follows behind, talking about all the years that have gone by, how much she loves Spencer and how sweet he is.

As she talks, I nod yeah, I know, I know, he's wonderful.

My coat and purse are on the kitchen counter. I pile them up and cut in on Slavka's adorations.

"Jo's sleeping," I say, "her bottle is in the refrigerator and I'll be back by one."

Slavka tilts her head from one side to the other, switching from the Spencer channel to the Jo channel.

"My Jo Jo," Slavka says, "I love my Jo Jo, she's so beautiful, she's so happy."

She follows me to the door and as I go, I nod to her music, agreeing that yes, Jo is so beautiful and so happy.

"See you in a little while," I say.

Slavka stops then.

"You so lucky, Jennifer," Slavka says, "your family is so beautiful."

I put my hand on Slavka's shoulder and kiss her on the cheek. The perfume she wears is a sweet mix of flowers.

"I'll see you in a little while," I say.

She lifts a hand to wave good-bye.

"Okay, Jen," she says, "bye-bye."

Out the door, I go to my car and get in behind the steering wheel. I shut the door and sit in the quiet for a long time.

May is in its full bloom now with the new green of the leaves in every tree. It's so pretty out here, it almost hurts my eyes to look at the colors. The whole place just bursts with new life.

I rub my hands up and down on my face and what I need is a cup of coffee and some advice.

I stop rubbing my face and start up the car.

Sugar Labs is an all-white place where the stylists wear white lab coats with little emblems stenciled on a right breast pocket that look like grains of sugar.

Mimi is one stylist who never wears a white lab coat, she goes for her own look, which changes based on her mood. She might be a punk rocker in leather and metal studs, romantic in lace and silk, or professional in a blazer and a pair of very snug-fitting capris. You never know with Mimi and I like that about her.

I walk through Sugar Labs with two cups of coffee and

Mimi's with a woman who sits with a black cape over her shoulders.

"Hi, stranger," I say.

"Jennifer!" Mimi says.

She leans to kiss me on each cheek, European style, and I love that about her too.

"I brought you a coffee," I say. "I thought it was time for a visit."

Mimi smiles with hot pink lips.

"Oh, honey," Mimi says, "thank you."

I put her coffee on the counter.

I sit in an empty chair nearby and it's one of those kinds that swivel side to side.

"How's that baby of yours?" Mimi says.

She goes back to cutting the woman's hair and Mimi is blue today, at least, her hair is blue. She's dyed the front a deep navy color and the rest of her hair is jet black.

"She's good," I say. "How about you? How have you been?"

"So busy," she says.

We talk around the woman in the chair and it hits me that I'm being so rude.

"I'm sorry," I say, "I'm Jennifer."

Mimi laughs and it's the loud, bar-room laugh of a girl who loves to have a good time.

"This is Marilyn," Mimi says. She pats the woman's shoulder. "Jen and I go way back, she's the one who wrote those books I told you about."

"Oh my goodness," Marilyn says, "of course. I remember."

There's a beat of quiet between the three of us and I push out the words I never use.

"Spencer is making me insane," I say. "I need some advice."

Mimi combs through Marilyn's long hair and nods in that way that says, "I'm listening."

"But maybe this isn't the right time," I say, "I don't want to interrupt your haircut."

Mimi shakes her head like that's just crazy.

"Forget it," she says, "Marilyn here has four kids and you know me, I always have the latest child information."

Mimi makes a big smile. She has a daughter who is three years older than Spencer and one of her favorite clients is a child psychologist. If anyone can help, Mimi can help, and I know it. Add Marilyn to the mix and it seems I'm in the perfect place.

Mimi cuts and I tell the whole story of Spencer's degeneration.

"When Jo was first born," I say, "he was great and I was so smug, but now he's losing it."

Mimi stops cutting Marilyn's hair and they both listen, a captive audience.

"He's still great with Jo, but he seems like he's so mad at me," I say. "I can't do anything right and the harder I try, the worse it gets and then today, on his birthday, I wanted it to be a nice morning and he's a pain, and then you know what he says? He says, 'I hate you, poop head.' "

It's all so funny and we laugh, but then I'm sad too. My son is just five and he already hates me. What's next? Therapy?

I stop laughing and shake my head.

"I am a terrible mother."

Mimi puts her comb and scissors in one hand and pats at my shoulder.

"Oh, Jennifer," Mimi says, "we're all terrible mothers."

Marilyn nods like, "Yes, it is true."

Mimi goes back to Marilyn and combs up a piece of her wet hair, starting to cut again.

"It sounds like the reality of the baby has finally kicked in," Mimi says.

"He probably just misses you," Marilyn says. "My son was that way when I had my second, he was so upset with me."

Mimi leans all her weight on one hip and shakes her comb over Marilyn's head the way she does when she wants to make a point.

"I don't even have a second kid and my daughter gets mad if I don't make special time," Mimi says. "We go out to dinner every Friday night."

"Oh, I remember," Marilyn says, "I'd take Darrin, that's my oldest, and we'd have a movie night together."

I'm not in on the conversation at all, the two of them figure it out between themselves and I sit back in the comfort of their voices.

It's true, Spencer *has* lost all the time we used to have, he has been forced from the center of the universe, and why wouldn't he be a little moody about that kind of change? It's normal. He's fine. I'm fine, but I don't know. It seems so simple somehow.

"It's a stage anyway," Mimi says, "he'll get over it."

"They always do," Marilyn says.

"Next problem?" Mimi says.

We laugh at Mimi and that's it. I have nothing else to say.

They go on talking together and I kick my heel against the footrest of the chair.

I know I should go home now and be with the baby or
maybe I should go get Spencer early from school and make it
up to him. I should do something that's about being a mother,
but I don't want to. I want to be here, in the comfort of other
women, other mothers.

Mimi dries Marilyn's hair and sprays a cloud of hairspray
to hold it all in place. Marilyn holds a mirror and looks at the
back of her hair, smoothing over it with her hand.

"You're a genius, Mimi," Marilyn says.

She gives Mimi the mirror and gets up from her chair.

There are good-byes and Euro kisses and Marilyn wishes
me good luck.

"Thanks," I say, "I need it."

"Oh no," she says, "you're doing fine."

"See you soon," Mimi says, and she waves until Marilyn is
out of earshot.

Mimi picks up the coffee I brought and sips, squinting one
eye at me at the same time.

"So," she says, "what are you working on?"

"Working on?" I say.

"Writing?" she says. "What are you writing?"

I look at her and she looks at me and I laugh out loud, but
Mimi doesn't laugh. She has her brows lifted in the question.

"I don't have time to write yet," I say.

Mimi takes another sip and her lipstick is pink around the
rim.

"I mean, I'm sketching out a few ideas, but the kids, the
house, Steve, you know," I say.

Mimi listens with this look that says I'm some kind of nut
and she clears her throat.

"Have you ever heard that our kids express our suppressed emotions?" she says.

I shift my coffee cup to one hand and bite at the edge of my nail.

"No," I say, "I haven't heard that."

"I don't know if it's true," Mimi says, "but I read that in a book so I gave it a try at home. When I'm pissed, my daughter is pissed. When I'm good, she's great."

She sets her coffee cup on the counter and crosses her arms.

"Check it out for yourself," she says. "You aren't working, you miss your work, you are going crazy not working, you probably hate yourself for not working and Spencer feels it, he's missing something, he's going crazy, and he hates you. Get it?"

Mimi leans her hip against the counter and I can see her and her back in the mirror. I'm in the mirror too but I don't want to see my reflection. I shift my eyes to look at Mimi straight on, except it doesn't matter. I can still see myself from the corner of my eyes.

"You're right," I say, "I know you're right. I am going crazy. I have to work."

"You've got help, right?" Mimi says.

"I do," I say, "I've got Slavka."

"And you can afford to pay her, right?" she says.

"I can," I say.

"You've got a breast pump," she says.

I laugh out loud and see myself laugh. God, it's good to laugh.

"I do have a great idea for a book," I say. "I've been making some notes in this journal."

"So get to work," she says, and then she puts her hand out, palm up.

"That'll be a hundred bucks," she says.

I stand then, putting my coffee next to Mimi's cup, and I press my hand into her hand, holding on tight.

"You're a good friend, Mimi," I say.

Mimi laughs like she knew all this and then she presses a real kiss on my cheek. I know she left a smear of pink lipstick on my face.

We say our good-byes and I walk through Sugar Labs, past the chairs with people who wear black capes and look at mirrors while stylists work on their hair. There is the sound of conversation all around, men and women chatting about nothing and everything, and I feel better, I feel like the weight isn't on my shoulders anymore, I feel like I have new things to think about and that I can rest easy on the idea that I've ruined my first pancake. I haven't ruined him. He's only five. He's barely started to cook.

At the door, I stop and look back to Mimi, but she's already chatting with another client. I can feel her lipstick on my cheek. Any other time I'd wipe something like that away but not today. I push through the door and let it close behind me, going to my car. I like the idea that Mimi has left her mark on me.

# IT TAKES A VILLAGE

The front porch of our house is up high from the sidewalk and from there, I can see our entire street with its houses and old trees. I can wave at our neighbors. I can watch the mail-woman come with her letters and packages. I can see Spencer play with other kids and call him back to the house.

This afternoon, I come out to the porch, and it's quiet in the neighborhood. Overhead, the sky is cloudy but clear and the street is covered with a blanket of white flower petals blown off the trees by a quick burst of wind.

"Spencer?" I yell.

"What?" he yells back.

"Where are you?"

"In the garage," he yells.

I hook the receiver of the baby monitor to my pants and go down our steps.

Across the street, two older boys lean against a tree. I know them, at least I've seen them on the street, but I can't be sure of their names. I think the blond one is Robert and the dark-haired one is Frank.

I wave in their direction.

"Hi, guys," I say.

The blond kid shoves off the tree and waves back.

The other one stays against the tree, looking off like he's thinking about things.

A tennis ball rolls down the driveway to stop in the gutter. Another tennis ball comes right behind, and then it's two more tennis balls, a basketball, and a neon orange soccer ball that has "Spencer" written all over in black ink.

Spencer's in the garage bent over a big bin of outside toys and the way he throws things reminds me of when he was a toddler and dumped all the stuff out of our drawers. It didn't matter which drawer, it could have been in the bathroom, bedroom, or kitchen. If he could reach the knob, he'd yank the drawer open and toss everything out. At first, it made me so mad. He had all these toys to play with, why did he insist on dismembering my drawers? Then, after picking up the mess a hundred times, I started to sort through the stuff in the drawers, getting it all organized in ways it never was organized before. I figured that's the way it was with kids. They were here to dig into places we didn't want to see. They were here to force us to clean up the mess.

Spencer is done with the bin of toys and moves on to the metal shelves.

"What are you doing?" I say.

"I'm looking for my sword," he says.

I step over broken pieces of sidewalk chalk, remote control cars, and a baseball mitt.

"What sword?" I say.

"My Nerf sword," he says.

I bend down to one knee, the plastic of the baby monitor digging into my side, and I sort through the mess on the floor.

"Spence," I say, "hand me that bucket in the corner, would you?"

"Mom," he says, "I need my sword."

"Bucket first," I say.

He grabs the bucket and drops it with a bang.

"Thank you," I say.

I throw in a piece of broken sidewalk chalk.

"Now why do you need your sword?"

"Because."

"Because why?"

"Because," he says, "we're going to kill someone."

I throw another piece of chalk into the bucket and my chest goes tight.

"Who is going to kill someone?" I say.

He nods at the boys across the way.

"Me and those guys," he says.

I rub green-and-pink chalk smears on my jeans. Every day, Spencer's got some version of a death trip where he talks about killing someone or being killed. There's pretend shooting that's all wrapped up in this ongoing war world of boys and it makes me crazy. If my mother friends even admit they have a boy like Spencer, most of them blow it off and say it's a "stage," like teething. By my calculations, Spencer's been in this stage for about three years now. When he was two, he fashioned his first gun from an empty paper towel roll.

"Spencer James," I say, "stop with the killing talk already. Besides, those boys are too old for you and you need to stay right here in front of the house."

Spencer gets all bendy at his knees, hands shaking like they are wet.

"We are playing in front of the house," Spencer says.

"They aren't in front of the house," I say, "and you are not crossing over because I can't see you over there, I need you close to me."

Spencer blows with a full-on fit. The tears roll out of his eyes, the snot pours, and I hate this scene almost as much as his killing mode.

I get off my knees and pull a roll of paper towels off the shelf.

"Look," I say, "it's enough, let me think here."

I yank off a paper towel and put it over his nose.

"Blow," I say.

Spencer honks into the paper towel and takes the fit to an inhaling, gulping sound.

I look from the boys, who lean together, to Spencer with tear lines down his cheeks.

"Come on," I say.

Spencer puts his hand into mine, still inhaling and gulping.

"Stop it," I say.

He takes it down to a sniff and we go down the driveway and to the curb.

Little white flower petals move under our feet as we cross over to the other side.

"Hey, guys," I say.

The blond kid stands up straight the way some kids do

when adults are around. The other kid, with the dark hair, stays all slouchy.

"You're Robert, right?" I say.

The blond kid nods.

"And you're Frank," I say.

The dark-haired kid nods.

"Where are your mothers?" I say.

Robert says his mom is at work and the baby-sitter is inside with his little brother, Frank says his mother lets him play on the street by himself.

"How old are you guys?" I say.

Robert says he's six and Frank says he's seven.

I hold up Spencer's hand in my own hand and this little arm wiggles between us.

"Spencer here is five."

I smile like we can all be friends, but there needs to be a few ground rules.

"If you all want to play, that's fine, but Spencer needs to stay in front of our house," I say, "and let's not kill anything or anyone today, why not just have a pretend sword duel and get a small cut?"

Robert smiles a little to himself and kicks at the sidewalk, but Frank doesn't smile. He looks very serious and I look at him extra hard.

"Okay, Frank?" I say.

When I say his name, he looks at me and nods a little nod.

Even though the boys are close in age to Spencer, they are different. Something about them makes me nervous, but I haven't been around enough older kids to know what the something is.

Spencer pulls from my hand then, but I keep ahold of him.

"Not so fast," I say, "you have to come back across."

We go to the curb together and Spencer looks over his shoulder.

"Come on, you guys," Spencer says.

The boys ignore him and huddle together again.

"They're not coming," Spencer says.

We stop at the curb and I look both ways before we cross.

"That's fine," I say, "we have to find your sword anyway."

Once across, I let go of his hand and go into the garage. Spencer stays at the curb and watches the boys with a naked longing that only kids allow themselves to show.

The Nerf sword is behind the rakes and shovels and it's this harmless pink-and-yellow thing made out of soft foam. I pull it by the tip and toss it on the sidewalk where it bounces at Spencer's feet.

"There you go," I say. "One sword."

Spencer picks it up by the handle and waves it side to side like a flag.

"I found it," he yells, "come on, come over."

I go back to the mess in the garage and on the baby monitor, Jo coos in her wake-up sound.

Across the street, the boys still ignore Spencer and his sword swings down to the ground, the tip trailing in the gutter.

I go to where he stands and bend so we are shoulder to shoulder, eye to eye.

"They aren't coming, Mom," he says.

I look over at the boys.

"They will, honey," I say, "or they won't, but that's okay,

you'll figure out something fun or you can come in the house with me and we'll play with Jo."

Spencer shakes his head.

"I don't want to be inside anymore," he says, "I want to play with the kids."

Jo's coos turn into a cry and I stand straight again.

"I'll try to find someone for you to play with," I say, "but you must stay here in front of the house."

I pull the baby monitor off my waistband and put my hand on Spencer's shoulder, pressing in to get his attention.

"I have to go in now," I say, "okay?"

Spencer kicks at the curb and nods.

"Okay," he says.

Over the next thirty minutes, I'm out to check on Spencer three times. Once, he was down at the corner with Robert and Frank and I had to call him back. Another time, he was around the corner with them and I had to call him back again, and then I pulled him away from those boys and sent him to play at the house of another little boy whose name is Malcolm. I didn't know Malcolm very well, but I knew he was a kid who liked to stay indoors and draw. How much harm could that be?

With Josephine up from her nap and fed, I come outside again.

Across the way, my neighbor Lori is on her front porch and she rocks her youngest on her lap and talks on the telephone at the same time. Her older girls are on the lawn turning cartwheels.

I go down the steps, pulling Jo's jacket over her small arms.

Lori comes down her steps too, still talking on the phone with her boy against her chest.

I cross the street and we meet at the bottom of her steps. She pushes a button to turn off the phone and puts her boy on his feet. He walks down the sidewalk barefooted, and then stops to look back at Lori.

"Stay close," she says.

Lori is a small woman with short brown hair, a pretty face, and eyes set wide. She's dressed like she's ready to go to the gym, in a sweatshirt with a hood and sweatpants. She pulls the waistband of her jacket down and smoothes herself out.

"How are you guys doing?" she says. "How's that baby of yours?"

She tickles one finger at Josephine, who is still sleepy faced from her nap, her soft hair whispering around her head like wind.

"We're good," I say. "How are you doing?"

"Oh, good," she says.

She looks past me to the street and puts her hands to her mouth.

"Car," she yells so loud I have to step back.

We watch the car drive by and I readjust Josephine in my arm.

"Spencer went down to play at Malcolm's," I say.

"Right," she says.

"I haven't really spent a lot of time with his parents," I say. "They're cool, right?"

Lori waves her hand at the air like she does.

"Very cool," she says, "they're musicians."

I nod, even though I don't get the connection between being good parents and being musical.

"I should check on him anyway," I say.

Lori does another wave-off thing.

"Oh, you worry too much," she says, "he's fine and besides, everyone on this street looks out for each other's kids, it's one of our rules."

I shift my weight side to side, rocking the baby.

"I know," I say, "it takes a village, right?"

"Right," she says, putting her hands on her chest, "we're the villagers and we look out for each other. So relax, he'll be fine."

I smooth Jo's coat over her tummy and I still want to check on Spencer, but I also want to believe the whole village thing.

I look toward Malcolm's house again, but lean up against the concrete of Lori's retaining wall. I shift Jo off my hip and onto my lap.

Lori's telephone rings then and she pushes a button on the handset.

Her little boy walks wobbly barefoot steps up their driveway and, since I'm a villager and all, I wonder if I should go help him.

"She's right here," Lori says.

Lori puts her phone between us.

"You have a call," she says.

"I have a call?"

"You have a call, it's Leslie."

"Leslie?"

Lori lifts the phone up at me.

"That's the one."

I move Jo to my hip again and take the phone. When I put the receiver to my ear, the black plastic holds the warmth of Lori.

"Jennifer?" Leslie says.

Leslie isn't part of the village, but she is another mother who lives a block away. She has a couple boys, Charlie and Cole, and Spencer likes to play with Cole. Leslie and I have had a few playdates but its been a long time.

Josephine whacks at the telephone and I move it to my other ear.

"It's me, Leslie," I say. "What's going on?"

Lori watches the street the way she does, but I can feel her questions about why I'm on her telephone.

On the phone, Leslie says she lost my number but knew I lived across the street from Lori and that this was an emergency.

"What's going on?"

Lori cups her hands over her mouth.

"Car!" she yells.

A couple of kids run from the middle of the street to the safety of the sidewalk and I hold the telephone closer.

"My nanny says Spencer was here with a knife," Leslie says.

"What?" I say.

Lori looks my way and Leslie laughs on the line except the sound of it is more like static. She goes on to tell this impossible story of how Spencer was at her house with two boys she didn't know and one of them had a knife. In all of this madness, Spencer said they wanted to kill Charlie.

"I am completely confused," I say. "My Spencer? Your Charlie?"

"That's right," she says.

"*My* Spencer was there?" I say.

"With two other boys," Leslie says.

"That is just impossible," I say, "he is over at another boy's house right now."

"No," Leslie says, "this was about forty minutes ago."

On the street, there's no sign of Robert or Frank.

It's quiet on the telephone and I just stand with Lori and the kids and the old houses and the old trees and all the white flower petals on the street and I can't move, I can't even think. I'm like the village idiot with Lori's phone in my hand.

Six months ago, we didn't live here.

Six months ago, I was still pregnant with Jo and we drove up this street covered with fall leaves.

Steve and I were up front and Spencer was safe in the backseat with his seat belt across his lap.

Steve pulled in front of a house with a wide run of concrete steps, a peaked roof, and a real estate sign that rocked in the breeze.

He shifted the car to park and draped his arm over the steering wheel, looking up at the house. He had this overflowing smile on his handsome face.

"Isn't it great?" Steve said.

I smiled for his happiness and put a hand over the round of the new baby inside me. Steve put his hand on top of mine, this stack of us on top of new life.

Across the street, three kids played and at the corner, a couple older boys kicked a ball.

"Look, Mom," Spencer said, "kids."

I turned in my seat and reached back to Spencer's knee.

"I see," I said.

"The real estate agent said there are twenty-three kids on this street," Steve said.

Across the way, the woman I'd know to be Lori came out of her house, talking on her telephone but looking at us at the same time.

"I want to play," Spencer said. "Can I get out, Mom?"

Steve sat back in his seat, turned the car off, and took the keys out of the ignition.

"We can all get out," Steve said.

I opened my car door then, my stomach leading the way, and Spencer worked the buckle for his seat belt.

"Hold on, Spence," I said, "let me help."

Lori came down her steps asking, "Are you the new neighbors?" and introduced herself. Steve shook her hand and the rest was like a blur. Lori called to a tall blond guy who was on his porch, "Come meet the new neighbors!" and he called to some other people from another house, "Come out here and meet the new neighbors!" and Steve and Spencer and I were surrounded with smiling faces and questions about who we were and where we came from.

In all the years I knew him, Steve always said he wanted his family in a quiet neighborhood where it was safe for the kids and where the neighbors would be our friends. He used to say it was both the American dream and his dream. From the way his face looked on that fall evening, it was like his dream had come true.

That night though, I had a dream.

In the dream, we were living in our new American-dream house and Spencer went to play with one of the kids. He was in their house and the kid had a gun and just like that, Spencer got shot in the head.

I opened my eyes on that dream and before I could calm

myself to how it was not real, tears were down the sides of my face and pooling in my ears. I squeezed my eyes tight, more tears spilling, and shook my head on the pillow. I wasn't going to let myself see the dream anymore, but the images of the gun and Spencer's lifeless body were too much. It wasn't the kind of dream I could forget.

Steve was next to me in the bed, but it wouldn't have helped to wake him up. For Steve, dreams just happened and he laughed them off as meaningless.

I shifted the covers off my body and went to check on Spencer.

In his room, the night-light sent shadows over his walls and floor.

Spencer was facedown, his arms grabbing at his pillow and his legs angled under his covers like he was trying to climb something. He had all his teddy bears around him, but his main bear, the one officially named Bear, was on the floor.

It was all I could do not to lie down and pull him into the curve of me, holding him as hard as I could.

I kneeled next to his bed instead, wiping my tears on the back of my arm. I picked up Bear, this big brown thing with huge patches of fur missing from his stomach and back. He had holes in his arms and legs and I had sewed him up so many times he was more like a patchwork bear.

Spencer breathed in deep, making this catch sound of a snore, and he moved his head up and down on the pillow, agreeing with something in his sleep.

With Bear in my lap, I moved my hand over Spencer's soft dark hair with such a light touch.

He had been in this room from the first day we brought him home from the hospital. He used to have his crib here, I changed all of his diapers here, and I nursed him in an old rocking chair, right here where I was kneeling now.

I remember holding him in my arms, this tiny new human, and I had forgotten what it was to love someone as much as I loved him. I once loved my own mother and father and brother that deep, but since they had all died, that kind of love was not allowed near my heart. I told myself that not even Steve was allowed near that place in me, but once Spencer came I had no choice. I was caught in this spell of love that ached in my soul. My love for him hurt worse because I knew that without warning, he could be taken from me. How could I live if something happened to my son?

Without an answer to that question, I went on, full of love and full of fear and it was easy. We lived on a busy street where the neighbors kept to themselves. The three of us were this island in our house and we watched one another carefully. Now it was going to get hard. We would move into that new house with its twenty-three kids and friendly neighbors and Spencer would want to go out and be among them. How could I watch him all the time? How could I possibly keep him safe?

They were the kind of midnight thoughts that made me feel so old.

Bear lay over my round stomach full of baby and I made myself take the dream apart to see all of its messages.

There was the gun, there was Spencer, there was Spencer getting shot in the head and how it was an accident, and the story of the dream dipped into the river of my past. Its details told the story of how my own brother found a gun when he was in college and shot himself in the head. Only my brother wasn't a little boy and his death wasn't an accident.

Dreams have a way of pulling things together from the past and from the present, they show what you're scared of and don't want to talk about. Dreams are like life, everything is interconnected, pieces of the past always touching the present and even the future, and we are here to sort them away from one another in a way that makes sense.

I was scared of death taking my child and I was scared to death of guns, and the dream hooked my fear into the death of my brother, which was something that I still could barely comprehend to this day.

Spencer moved in his bed, turning from his stomach to his side, and his face was lit up by the shadows of the night-light, his small nose, his soft cheeks, his long eyelashes around the hollows of his eyes. I watched him for such a long time and then I put Bear back in bed with him, tucking him close to Spencer's body. I kissed his face, smelling that wonderful, clean little-boy smell, and then I made myself go back to bed.

I run up the block with Josephine bouncing on my hip and at Malcolm's front door, I ring the bell over and over.

Past the screen is a glass door with cream-colored sheers and through the sheers, there is a staircase that leads up.

I pull open the screen door and knock on the glass with my knuckles.

"Come on," I say to the closed door, "answer the door."

I see myself reflected in the glass, Josephine on my hip like a forgotten accessory.

Inside, a little boy comes to the door and uses both hands to pull it open.

"You're Malcolm, right?" I say.

"Yeah," he says.

I balance the screen door on my hip.

"Do you remember me?" I say, "I'm Spencer's mom."

Malcolm has long bangs, almost into his eyes, and he moves his hand up in his hair and blows up at the same time like he's winded or just worn out.

"I know that," he says.

"Sure you do," I say, "I'm sorry. Spencer's here, right?"

He waves me in and does the thing with his bangs again.

"We're making a comic book," he says. "Come on in."

I step over the threshold and let the screen door close behind me.

"Your mom is here," Malcolm yells and that fast, Spencer stomps out of the kitchen with a mad look on his face.

I want to hug him, I want to shake him, I want to yell at him, and I want to start crying. I move Josephine against my side and put my hand out in his direction.

"We've got to go," I say.

"Mom," he says, stopping a few feet off. "I want to play."

"Spencer," I say. "You have played enough, now it's time to talk."

Any other time, Spencer would go into a fit, but he must know there's trouble because he lifts a hand to Malcolm.

"See ya," he says.

"Yeah," Malcolm says, "see you around."

Outside again, the village is in full swing. All the neighbors are out on the sidewalk, chatting with one another. Kids ride bikes and chase each other.

At our house, Steve is just home from work and he stands

next to his car, talking to Lori, who holds her son at her hip.

When he sees me he waves and I wave back, but I toss him a chin-up thing that says, "We've got trouble."

Steve gets the message loud and clear and he comes inside with us.

"What's going on?" he says.

I close the door, us on the inside, the village on the outside.

"Let's sit," I say.

When I was a kid, my parents didn't have conversations with me. The talking went on behind closed doors while I waited in my room and then the belt came out. Steve's childhood was just about the same.

We're different though, we're enlightened. We don't hit our children. We strive to be reasonable and fair.

Steve sits in a big wing chair, Spencer's on the sofa, and I'm on the floor with Josephine, who lies on her baby blanket.

Afternoon sun comes in through the windows at the back of the house, and even though the front door is closed there is the sound of kids and Lori yelling, "Car!"

"Tell us what happened over at Cole's house today," I say.

Spencer's face goes blank like he has no idea, and then his eyes get wide. He's not old enough to have clear diction and his words come out mashed together like he has marbles in his mouth. He does a good job telling it anyway. Frank had a knife, they wanted to show it to someone, and then Spencer thought it would be fun to go over to his old friend Cole's house.

"Frank said it would be okay," Spencer said, "and he taught me how to play doorbell ditch."

Jo is on her back and she rolls one way and then the other.

In the second telling, the story is just as bad as it was when I heard it from Leslie, but I'm calming down. Steve's hearing it for the first time though and he uncrosses his legs to put both feet on the floor.

I push my hair back from my face and tuck it behind my ear.

"Okay," I say, "so you went over to Cole's house, without asking me?"

"Frank said it was okay."

"Who is in charge," I say, "me or Frank?"

Spencer drops his chin to his chest and slumps deeper into the sofa.

"You are," he says.

Steve moves his hand over his mouth and rubs the five o'clock shadow on his chin.

"How big was this knife?" he says.

Spencer holds his hands open and according to him, this knife is butcher-size.

"One that folded?" Steve says, "like a pocket knife?"

Spencer nods like yes.

Steve puts his hands together, keeping still in his version of reasonable, and then he sets his sights on me.

"How did this happen?" Steve says.

"Excuse me?" I say.

"Weren't you watching him?" Steve says.

I clear my throat.

"I was, but he was on his own too," I say. "I told him to stay in front of the house."

Josephine reaches up and I put my fingers into her hands.

"Why wasn't he in here with you?" he says.

Jo locks her hand tight on my fingers and pulls to sit.

In my stomach is a tight wind-up feeling I get when we are about to have a fight.

"He wanted to be outside, Steve," I say.

"Sometimes he can't be outside," Steve says. "Someone has to watch him."

Spencer kicks his heels up and down against the sofa and his arms are wide over the cushions. He looks like a coat that was tossed on the sofa and forgotten.

"Look," I say, "you weren't here with him today. It's summer, he's crazy to play with kids, and I had to let him out. I told him to stay in front of the house, I checked on him every ten minutes, what else could I do?"

Steve does this shake of his head that says I really screwed up.

Jo pulls to stand, still holding my fingers. Her knees give in and she lands back on her bottom.

My whole body is tense and mad, but I don't want to be mad with Spencer here, I sure don't want to fight with Steve, but there is no way around it.

"You can blame me for this, Steve, but this is part of the American dream," I say. "This is what happens when we live where there are lots of kids. Some of those kids have knives, some of them might have guns and light fires and have fights."

Steve looks at me and I look at him.

"There wasn't a fire," Spencer says.

Steve looks at Spencer and I look at him too, and we can't help it, we laugh then.

"And we were just kidding," Spencer says, "it was a joke."

Steve rubs his whole face then and shakes his head.

"I just can't believe this would happen here," he says, "it seemed like such a nice neighborhood."

Josephine reaches for a stuffed lion that's just beyond her fingers and I get it for her.

"It is a nice neighborhood, Steve," I say, "but this kind of thing happens and we have to deal with it."

I can't believe I'm being so reasonable. Any other time, this would be a huge fight. I would be filled with doubt that I made some terrible mistake, I'd try to defend myself to Steve or even try to make him agree with me. None of that happens. Inside, I know I could have kept Spencer in the house, but this is life. It's full of knives and messes and lessons. Thank God this one wasn't that painful. Thank God everyone is safe.

I put a plan together for Steve to talk to Frank and Robert's parents, and for us to talk about this with all the parents on the street.

"I'll take Spencer to Leslie's house and he will apologize to her and Charlie," I say.

Steve sits back in the big chair and nods at my plan.

"What about discipline?" he says, nodding at Spencer.

I stand up then and put Josephine into Steve's lap.

"We'll talk about it when we get back," I say.

I put my hand out in Spencer's direction.

"Come on, Spence, let's go."

Twenty minutes later, Spencer and I walk hand in hand and behind us is Leslie's house and Spencer's apology.

"I'm sorry I said I wanted to kill Charlie," Spencer said. "We were just kidding."

"Thank you, Spencer," Leslie said and she smiled, but who knew what was past that smile. She probably thinks I'm raising some kind of murderer and I don't know, maybe I am.

Walking together now, I can't help think of the dream I had all those months ago. I can't help fit the pieces together and I see that it's the violence of boys that I've been hiding from. I hate it, I want it to go away but it's not going away. It's here and I wonder if this is how it all started with the boy who grew up to take a gun to school and kill his classmates or the one who shot his parents while they slept. Were those boys like my sweet Spencer? Did they have knives when they were seven and start with doorbell ditch and death threats? In ten years, will he graduate to making bombs from directions off the Internet or stockpiling guns? One day, will I be the mother on the news who looks at the camera and says, "I don't know what happened, he was such a sweet kid."

Elm and maple trees line the street and they are heavy with green leaves. The air smells like rain. I let go of Spencer's hand and touch over his head, stopping to rest on his shoulder. He's so small.

"Once when I was five," I say, "my dad pulled down my pants and spanked me with his belt."

Spencer tilts his face up and his eyes are so wide, so dark, and so serious.

"Why?" he says.

I shrug my shoulder.

"I can't remember," I say. "I think my brother and I were making too much noise while my mother was sleeping."

Spencer puts his attention down the sidewalk.

"Am I getting a spanking?" he says.

I stop and Spencer stops too.

"Do you think I should spank you?" I say.

Spencer shakes his head side to side.

"No," he says, "we don't spank."

"Why don't we spank?" I say.

"Because," he says, "hitting is wrong."

"That's right," I say.

I squeeze his shoulder and pull him closer to my side. We walk again and up ahead is the intersection.

Wind blows the leaves in the trees and the sound is like a polite audience clapping after a performance.

At the crosswalk, we stop and a car goes by. I bend over at my waist to look at him at his level.

"A lot of things are wrong, Spencer," I say. "Leaving our block without telling me is wrong. Talking about killing is wrong, even if it's a game. Playing with knives is wrong and the next time you see one, you have to tell me or another grown-up."

I keep my eyes steady on his eyes the way I do when it's serious.

"Do you understand me?"

Spencer nods like yes, he understands.

I stand up then and offer my hand. He puts his hand into mine and we cross the intersection.

"So what are we going to do for a punishment?" I say. "What do you think is fair?"

Spencer kicks his foot against the curb as he steps up to the sidewalk on the other side.

"No dessert," he says, "and no TV."

"For tonight?" I say, "or for a few days?"

"For tonight and tomorrow night," he says.

"Do you think that's fair?" I say.

He tilts his head to the side, looking at the sky over my head, and then back at me.

"Yes," he says, "that's fair."

"Okay," I say.

We are under a long row of big old chestnut trees, the trunks so big I could put my arms around them and my hands still wouldn't touch.

There are so many things I want to say to him right now. I want to tell him about the dream. I want to tell him about my brother and how he made a terrible mistake with a gun. I want to tell him how dangerous the world is in general. I want to tell him how scary this day was, how he could have been killed or killed someone or hurt himself or another person and that, one day, it could be a gun or a bomb or a fire. I want to tell him to be careful, to be safe, and to learn how to look out for himself because, in the end, I can't.

At the corner, we turn onto our block and Spencer pulls his hand free.

"Can I run the rest of the way home?" he says.

"Okay," I say.

He takes off with arms and legs pumping, elbows and knees bending, and his chin out like an arrow, pointing him in the direction he wants to go.

I didn't say everything I want to say, but I will. I'm still afraid of his violent world, but I won't wait for him to grow out of this stage. I'm going to watch him close and try to stay wide awake.

That warm, sweaty feeling of our touch is on my skin and I close my fingers into my palm.

Our village is quiet now, all the kids and grown-ups are in

their houses for the night and the white flower petals that were all over the street have been shoved into the gutters by the wind and the passing cars.

At our house, Spencer disappears up the steps and I hear him yell, "Dad, I'm home."

I walk the rest of the way alone with my hand closed tight, as if I can hold on to the feeling of Spencer forever.

# BUBBLES

In the sink, bits of chicken and rice float in hot water and soap bubbles. I scrub a dish, rinse it clean, and put it into the rack.

"Da," Josephine says. "Da, da, ta, ta."

She leans on a stack of plastic bins, balancing herself to stand with one hand, while with the other she pulls a towel from a stack of folded towels. She throws it on the ground, offended by stacks and folds.

We all call her Jo Jo, like the potato, since she's this tiny but solid wedge of a person. She has golden curls and blue eyes as clear and round as the really good marbles I had as a kid.

Overhead is the sound of hard hammers hitting home. Sawdust shakes from the light fixture to rain down on my head, the dishwater, the clean dishes, and Jo.

"Damn it," I say.

With the sound of my voice, Josephine stops tearing things up and puts her blue marble eyes on me.

I wipe my hands dry on a towel and bend to dust off her shoulders. She's so sturdy under my touch and she's never been one of those babies who lay on her back, cooing and kicking for months on end. From the moment she entered the world, I felt the power of her will in her strong body. She was holding her own head up by one month, rolling over by two and a half months, and crawling at four months. At eight months, she is pulling herself up, and soon, she'll be walking.

Sometimes I want to say, "Slow down, you have lots of time," but Jo has something in her own mind, she has a destination to reach and perhaps, deep in the abyss of her soul, she feels encumbered by her infancy. She is so dead set to go, it's like she believes her last life is double-parked somewhere and that she can grow up fast enough to climb back in and drive off to her original destination.

I pick sawdust out of her hair and she stays still with my touch.

"There you go, baby," I say.

I dust my own shoulders and take the dishes out of the strainer to start over again.

Down here in the basement is a washer, a dryer, a short counter, and the sink in between. There's a hole in the wall behind me where the construction guys put in a new water heater, and in the wall just over the sink there's an empty electrical panel with exposed wires. There is a bit of space at the opposite end of the room for the microwave and a hot plate and there's a cubbyhole for the refrigerator and the bins for storing food.

Upstairs is the kitchen except it's gone now, torn down to studs. For the next three months, we're in a construction zone.

Josephine pulls out a package of ramen, the crinkle sound

of the plastic under her hand as she throws the pack on top of the towels.

I rinse the dishes a second time and put them back in the strainer.

Since we don't have windows down here, I've taped up a bunch of Spencer's school art around the holes in the Sheetrock.

One is a drawing of a huge motorcycle.

"That's me," he said, pointing out the smiling circle balanced on the seat of the hog.

There's another drawing of a stick person with long lines for legs, very short lines for arms, and in one of those arms a tiny circle with a smile.

"That's you," he said, "holding Jo."

I love Spencer's art.

There is no more noise from upstairs and I look at my watch. The workers must be calling it quits. Thank God, I can't take any more hammering and dust tonight.

Josephine drops to her hands and knees and crawls like a spider to the tub of plastic containers. She pulls herself up and looks my way, making sure I'm not going anywhere. I smile at her. "Yep, I'm still here."

I wipe my hands on a towel and take an empty container off the floor.

"Can I have this one, Jo Jo?" I say.

She looks into the bin of plastic containers, as if searching, and I reach around her, pulling out a plastic lid that fits.

"Got it," I say.

I take a pan off the burner and scoop out the leftover mac and cheese. It's congealed together, milk and cheese and macaroni shells, and makes a *thunk* as it hits the plastic container.

My hands shake a little with a nervous thing I get when there are a hundred tasks to do.

Things are getting better here, at least I'm working again, but the scales are still tipped to the house, to the kids, to Steve, and there never seems to be enough time to get it all done before someone yells that they need something.

From the way she keeps looking my way every few seconds, that someone is going to be Josephine next. In about five more minutes, she'll be at my ankles and tugging on my pants to be picked up.

I pull the plug in the sink and the water drains through the bits of food stuck in the strainer with a sucking sound. There are a couple of forks and spoons in the bottom of the sink and I turn the water on again, adjusting the nozzle of the faucet from spray to stream.

The water hits one of the spoons and bounces back up in a fountain that sprays my shirt, the counter, and the wall behind the sink.

"Darn it," I say.

Water spray hits Spencer's motorcycle art, bleeding the blue ink, and I dab at it with a towel.

Josephine drops to all fours and crab crawls to my feet. She pulls herself up, tiny hands fisting my skin and my pants, and then she presses her face into my knee.

"Oooooh," she says in that feel-good sound you make when you lie down in your safest and most comfortable place.

"Hang on, honey," I say, wringing out a washcloth. There is still so much left to do.

"Ahhhhh," she says and it's her sound that says, "I don't wait."

With dripping hands, I bring her up to my hip and she lays her head on my shoulder and says "ooooooh" again.

Before I ever had kids, there was a woman who told me I would never be able to keep up the house and take care of my kids. She said something would have to go and it should be the house. "Let the house go," she said, "enjoy your kids."

Comments like that used to really piss me off. I liked to believe I could do it all and most of the time I did, but I'm changing. I'm actually giving in, in spite of myself. I'm just tossing the towel on the edge of the counter and saying forget it. The dishes aren't getting done, the rest of the house is a mess, and this baby needs to be up in my arms.

I pat her on the back and check my watch. I wish time would give in too but time doesn't stop, it just ticks on and now it's bath time and bedtime.

"Let me make a bottle and we'll get Spencer."

Jo lifts her head off my shoulder and her blue eyes search the laundry room.

"Ta, ta," she says.

She points her finger to the empty doorway as if saying, "Let's go find him now."

There's a tunnel that runs through the basement and out of the garage. It's cold and damp and smells of wet concrete. I duck as I go through, Jo Jo on my side, and at the other end, I push the automatic door opener with my elbow.

There is the sound of the chain that pulls the door up and evening sunlight fills the garage.

Outside, it's an Indian summer night with golden leaves that still hang in the trees. I squint and Jo Jo does it too, her small nose pulled into a wrinkle.

I go to the end of the driveway and stop at the curb.

Josephine makes a high squeal sound and points across the street.

Spencer is on the other side with Charles, except no one calls him that. On this street, everyone calls him Pau, which is Hawaiian for "done." Since he's the last of four kids, I guess the name fits.

For the longest time, I thought it was Pal, not Pau, which was just right for me since Pau was Spencer's first pal when we moved here a year ago. Pau or Pal or Charles, it doesn't matter what you call him, he's a sweet kid who loves to play with Spencer and doesn't even mind how Spencer bosses him around.

Spencer's over there chatting it up and he turns a bucket upside down into his wagon, dumping a load of chestnuts they've been collecting.

"Spencer," I yell, "it's time to come in."

He turns the bucket upright again and looks my way.

"I just got out here," he yells.

"You've been out here for an hour," I say. "Now it's time to come in."

Spencer looks at Pau for support, but Pau stays extra still, arms by his sides the way kids get when they know grown-ups are serious.

"I don't want to come in," Spencer yells.

"Spencer," I say, "you are coming in."

Spencer stomps his foot.

"No," Spencer says.

I look at Jo, who looks at me, and I clear my throat to make my most serious grown-up voice.

"Spencer James," I say, "get over here right now."

Spencer crosses his arms.

"No," he says.

I roll my lips together, working to keep my cool even as it slips away. I cross the street to where they are and I look at Spencer, at Pau, and then at Spencer again.

"Spencer has to come in now," I say, "we'll see you tomorrow, Pau."

"Okay," Pau says.

Pau pushes his hands into his pockets and heads up the sidewalk to his house.

"Bye, Spencer," Pau says.

Spencer unfolds himself and does a deep kneebend.

"No," Spencer yells. "I don't want to come in, I want to play."

"You can play tomorrow," I say.

"NO-OOOO!" Spencer howls.

Pau is three houses away and he looks back at us just for a second and keeps going. With my free hand, I take the wagon handle and do a good job of being calm even though in my head, I wonder, Why is my child this way? Pau doesn't throw a fit like this, I've never seen him melt down, only my son seems to go nuts and he only seems to do it with me. Why? Why? Why?

"Come on, Spence," I say, "you have to cross with me."

It's slow going, but Spence comes, crying and shaking his head and kicking at the street. I get the wagon into the garage, close the door, and go up the front steps to the main door. Spencer is ten steps back, his cries mixed with, "I never get to play, you never let me do anything!"

I want to throw my own fit, I want to stomp my foot and

say, "Okay, I'm here, I'm putting you first, I'm not taking care of the house or me or anything else. Now, come on, pay up. Where's the good stuff? How is this fun for me?"

Of course, I don't.

At the top of the steps, I lean against one of the stone pillars and shift Jo to sit on its flat top.

Our street is littered with spiky seedpods split down the middle and thousands of those brown chestnuts, but overhead, the sky is a clear blue with clouds shaded pink.

Two bottles of bubbles are open near where Jo sits and I reach for the lids to close them up.

I don't know why, it's not my way to get all playful, especially with Spencer so upset, but the bubbles are too tempting. Instead of putting the lid on, I put my finger into one of the bottles and fish out a wand.

Spencer stops at the top of the landing and tear lines streak his dirty face.

Water and soap are thick on the wand and I blow. Out the other side of the plastic circle, a mismatch of bubbles unfold and float.

Josephine laughs and the sound is as light and as clear as the bubbles themselves.

I open my eyes wide at Spencer like, "Wow, did you hear that," and even though he doesn't want to, he lets go of his frown and lets a smile lift.

"She laughed," he said.

"I know," I said.

I dip the wand into the soap again and the next run of bubbles is better than the first and so is Jo's laugh. The sound of her is deep from her gut and it's so good, it's like hearing music for the first time.

Spencer laughs too and I remember how great it was to hear him laugh when he was about her age. His sound was deep and in his throat.

He comes up the last three steps and I give him the other bottle of bubbles.

Together, we are dedicated to the cause of making her laugh more. We dip, we blow, we listen to her crack up, and then we do it all again.

Jo giggles so hard tears run down her face and she holds a hand over her stomach, like, "No, I can't take anymore."

"Isn't she funny?" I say.

Spencer laughs too, not at the bubbles, but at Jo. Spencer laughs so hard, he holds his own side with his hand and his eyes lift in the corners.

Children express our suppressed emotions. Isn't that what my friend told me a few months back? Here I was, irritated and frustrated and under the gun to get things done, and there was Spencer, freaking out for no reason at all. You could say it was his own thing, his own fit, his own little head game of control, or you could say he's hardwired into my body and just letting the feelings flow since I won't. But now we are here, blowing bubbles and having the best time ever. I don't know what time it is. I don't even care.

Spencer laughs and I laugh and Jo is between us, laughing her music and clapping her hands to keep time. She's like a Buddha. Among us, with her golden glow, she's brought us to the light just by being in our world. I wonder if that is one of the purposes of her willful soul or if it's just something we get to enjoy before she masters her body and hits the road.

# LIFE IS WHAT HAPPENS

It's half past seven on a Wednesday morning and I'm on the sofa with Josephine cradled in my arm.

Spencer's still in PJs and he's a green Power Ranger, one of those invincible superheroes. He's cross-legged on the rug, crashing a Spiderman action figure into a Buzz Lightyear action figure, his mouth sputtering and spitting.

I pull up my shirt, unsnap my bra, and move the baby into position for the latch on, suck, and takeoff of breast-feeding. At the same time, I make my voice low in this whisper that sometimes catches Spencer more than saying a thing out loud.

"Spencer," I say, "I have a deal for you."

Spencer looks my way.

"If you get yourself dressed and brush your teeth," I say, "I'll take you out for breakfast."

"Starbucks?" Spencer says.

"You bet," I say, "but you gotta fly, baby. Go, go, go."

Spencer drops Buzz and Spiderman and is up the stairs like a greyhound after a rabbit. Nothing says fun more than a muffin in a bag and juice in a box.

Josephine pops off to watch Spencer run away and in the quiet of the living room, she moves her big blue eyes to my face.

"Isn't Mommy smart?" I say.

I ease her back on and Jo makes her happy baby sucking sounds, like my milk is nectar from the gods. I let my head fall back on the sofa and close my eyes.

There is this commercial on television where a woman wakes up in the morning and picks up a briefcase, a baby bottle, her son's lunch box, and all these other things and juggles them over her head. She goes through her whole day that way, from home to office and back home again, actually juggling these things until she lies down in bed and puts all of the things down. It's not the insanity of the woman's existence that gets me, it's the calm on her face. It's this serene calm you'd see on the surface of a lake at dusk, as if mastery of chaos is her purpose in life.

She's either my role model or my worst nightmare, but I can't figure out which one yet.

Josephine opens her mouth and lets me go, a satisfied look on her round baby face.

I dab around her mouth with her baby blanket and snap myself back together.

I get off the sofa and my legs are heavy the way they get when they are completely relaxed. I move Jo against my shoulder, the soft warmth of her pressed into me, and pat air bubbles out of her stomach.

I push my feet into slide-on shoes and open the front door.

The day is wet and the leaves in the trees are heavy with the last wave of rain.

On the porch, there's a paper wrapped in blue plastic to save it from the rain. It's another paper I won't read, but I pull it from its plastic anyway, shutting the door with my hip. The paper inside is bound with a round of elastic. I take the rubber band off and toss the paper on the floor.

"Spencer," I yell. "How are you doing?"

He moves around up there but there's no answer.

I stop in the hall where we have a mirror on the wall. I lean on the doorjamb across from the mirror, squat with my knees together to make my body into a chair, and balance Josephine in my lap. I pull my hair together, make a ponytail, and hold it in place with the rubber band. The ponytail is a mess and I am a grizzly sight. I have on black stretch pants that I've worn every day this week and my shirt is one of those oversize long-sleeved things with holes under the arms.

I had a friend who once said it was just as easy to look nice as it was to look like shit. Of course, she said this when we were single. We said a lot of stupid things back then.

I have a deal with myself now, no obsessing about appearances or weight until the baby is done nursing. The look of horror on my face breaks my deal. It's the one I've had my entire life, that mean-spirited critic who says, "You are too fat, lose some weight."

I move Josephine into my left arm and push off the doorjamb, walking away from that look and the thirty extra pounds that shiver around my butt.

"Spencer," I yell, with an extra kick of anger, "come on, man, we gotta go."

I cross through the kitchen and then the dining room, stepping over toys, a mega-size box of diapers, and the baby's bouncy chair. The counters and tables are covered with newspapers, mail, diapers, and baby wipes. The floors are dirty, dust bunnies curl in the corners, and I don't even want to think about the smell in the bathroom. As I go by, I close the door.

I get the baby's shoes, socks, and coat off the windowsill in the hall and stop my travels at the bottom of the staircase that leads up. The upstairs bathroom door is closed and I should hear the whir of a Mickey Mouse toothbrush, but instead there are banging doors sounds, like cabinets being opened and closed.

"Spencer!" I yell.

"I'm done," he yells back.

He opens the bathroom door and turns off the light.

As he comes down the steps, he's transformed from a green Power Ranger to a little boy in jeans and a red T-shirt with a black handprint on the front.

I balance all my weight on one leg and get Josephine tight against my side.

"Look at you," I say.

Spencer stops two steps up from me, his hand on the rail, and leans over to blow air into my face.

"Fresh breath," he says.

"It is fresh," I say.

He moves his hand over his head, smoothing slicked-down hair.

"And look," he says. "Gel."

"Wow," I say, "where did you get hair gel?"

"From the cabinet," he says, "and smell."

He goes up on his toes and tilts his head back, showing me all of his neck.

"Cologne," he says.

He's an entire perfume counter at a department store and it's all I can do not to step back.

Josephine's face spreads open in a wide grin and her hands wave at Spencer like he's the greatest thing. Her complete celebration of his existence melts my grown-up standards of good taste.

"You look and smell wonderful," I say. "Josephine even thinks so."

Spencer gets all puffed up in his chest and comes the rest of the way down the steps.

"Yeah," he says, "I know."


Fifteen minutes later, Spencer runs down the sidewalk and stops at the door of the coffee shop. He digs his heels in and uses both hands to pull open the glass door.

Josephine is in my left arm, her back against my upper arm and her bottom balanced on my forearm in the quarterback football hold.

"Who's a cute little cutie?" I say, "you are a cute little cutie, yes you are, yes you are."

I have no idea why I talk this way, it could be the high that comes after nursing or the fact that she really is cute, or how I've always been chatty in the presence of a person who won't carry her side of the conversation.

Spencer waits for us, the door balanced at his back, and I go in ahead of him.

There isn't a mother or a child in the place. "Thank you, sir," I say.

The coffee shop is filled with the feeling of grown-ups on their way to work. It's all executive suits and women in panty-hose and heels, real world people who've had showers, who read newspapers, and who talk on their cell phones with "I'm so busy" looks on their faces.

Just being among all this professional energy makes me snap into the model of a woman who is more in control than she is and who needs to manage her children in a way that doesn't disturb the professional mood or slow anyone down. I set my face like the juggling woman in the commercial, I'm serene, I'm calm, I've got it all under control.

Spencer runs ahead and gets in line in front of a suit. The man inside the suit regards Spencer like he's not a little boy, but rather a dog that got in by mistake.

I ease Spencer out of the line.

"Be polite, Spencer," I say, "we need to get in the back."

At the back of the line, we wait behind six people and more people come behind us, this flood of humans craving caffeine.

"I want a cinnamon roll," Spencer yells.

I put my finger to my lips and bend close to his ear. His cologne stings my nose.

"Inside voice, please," I say. "You can have a cinnamon roll, but you need to have the fruit cup too."

"Yuck," Spencer says, "I hate fruit."

I stand up tall, serene mother smile on my face.

"You decide," I say.

Spencer shifts his weight from one foot to the other, weighing his next move.

"Fine," he says, "but I want chocolate milk too."

He leans into the cold case next to the register and picks out a carton of chocolate milk. I try to intercept but he pulls the milk away.

"No," I say. "Juice today."

"I hate juice," he says and stomps his foot.

"Spencer," I say, "put it back."

"No," he says.

"May I help you?" the lady behind the counter says.

She has on a green apron and a smile that holds just the bottom of her face.

If I could get ahold of Spencer, I'd shake him good, but I take the debate into my head instead.

Milk is fine, it has vitamins and calcium, so what if he's high-wired on sugar, it's a fair trade.

Spencer tugs my pants leg.

"Pleeeese," he says.

"Fine," I say, "take the milk and sit at that table, right there by the window, but do not open the milk until I get there."

With my free hand, I scoot Spencer in the direction of the table and readjust the baby in my arm.

I make my order and she punches away at the keys.

"That's seven fifty," she says, and the numbers come up on the big screen between us.

"Mom," Spencer yells.

I step out of line and over at the window is the table where Spencer should be and a puddle of chocolate milk. Spencer is at the condiment counter with a dysfunctional napkin dispenser, napkins piled around his feet. His face is full of tragedy and the last bit of calm is gone from mine.

"Oh, Spencer," I say, shaking my head. "Hang on, I'm coming."

I dig into my wallet for the cash, but on my hand, my arm, and all over my wallet there's a warm run of baby goo.

Josephine is cradled in my arm, oblivious to air bubbles or barf or bad timing. She smiles into her round cheeks like life is great.

"Oh, Jo Jo," I say.

Of course, I don't have a napkin or a beach towel, and now there are so many people behind us, they have to file out the side door and onto the sidewalk, every single one of them looking as if we are making them incredibly late for the meeting that will seal the deal, save the day, and change the world as we know it.

Three people back is a woman who is a little younger than I am, maybe somewhere in her midthirties. She has blond hair swept up and held in place with a little clip and she wears a pressed powder blue business suit. She has sparkly diamond studs in her earlobes and a fresh "I've slept all night" quality to her flawless face.

Perhaps she's a newlywed.

Perhaps she's been considering children.

Perhaps she's even flush with the recent news that she is, in fact, pregnant.

This woman looks as if she can't quite believe what she sees, her soft blue eyes so wide, they might pop right out of her pretty head.

The look in her eyes is pure fear and I don't blame her a bit.

My juggling act is over. The balls are on the floor. I am the poster of the anti-mother who makes the case for contraception or possibly sterilization.

Didn't John Lennon write, life is what happens when you're busy making plans?

On a Wednesday morning in a coffee shop in Portland, Oregon, and this is life and this is motherhood. It's not a commercial. This is reality TV. I'm a disaster and I'm doing it, all at the same time.

I laugh out loud since I have no choice. What could be more hysterical than the chaos of these kids and all that has gone wrong with them in such a short space of time. More than that, isn't it going to be boring when they are bigger and serious, like all the professional people in this place. I hope they never turn out that way.

I laugh hard and the sound catches the woman behind the counter, her face going from half to a whole smile.

She hands over a bar towel.

"Thanks," I say.

"You've got your hands full," she says.

I wipe the baby barf off my wallet and give the lady a ten-dollar bill. I use the side of my arm to wipe the tears off my face.

"It's true," I say.

I wipe her counter down and leave the towel on her side of the counter.

"I don't think I'd have it any other way," I say.

She hands me my change and nods, but not in the way that shows she gets what I mean. She's already looking past me to the next customer, but it doesn't matter, I'm getting it finally.

With Jo against my side, I get out of the line and head to the condiment counter to rescue Spencer.

Printed in the United States
88403LV00001B/175-180/A